Life After
Graduation

Your Guide to Success

Terry Arndt & Kirrin Coleman

A Life After Graduation, LLC Publication

P.O. Box 11205 ✦ Bainbridge Island WA 98110

Info@LifeAfterGraduation.com

www.LifeAfterGraduation.com

COPYRIGHT INFORMATION

BOOK DISCLAIMER

ACKNOWLEDGMENTS

I would like to acknowledge and thank the thousands of colleges, students, and private organizations who have made my company a success. I would also like to acknowledge and thank the following reviewers and businesses for their insightful suggestions regarding the development of *Life After Graduation:*

Jeanette Alexander
Owner
Jeanette Alexander Graphic Design

Karolyn Bald
Student Services Coordinator,
Career Services
University of Wisconsin, La Crosse

Cady Bar
Campus Relations Manager
Vector Marketing Corporation

Jenna Belknap
Campus Recruiter
BDO Seidman, LLP

Natalie Bounds
Alumni Relations Director
Oral Roberts University

Jane G. Colson
Director, Career Resources
Eckerd College

Scott Crawford
Director of Career Services
Wabash College

Sheila Curran
Executive Director,
Duke University Career Center
Duke University

Lorie A. Davis
Alumni Career Services
Shippensburg University of
Pennsylvania

Rachel Eddins
Career Counselor, University Career Services
University of Houston

Patricia Gaynor
Assistant Director, Career Center
Senior Year Transition and Employment
Programs
California State University, Northridge

Jeana Gingery
Program Coordinator
Krell Institute

Patricia Gochenauer
Assistance Director,
Career Development Center
Shippensburg University of Pennsylvania

Gary Howarth
Owner
Howarth Financial Services, LLC

Bonnie J. Jerke, MA, GCDF, MCDP
Director of Career Services
George Fox University

Beth Johnson
Career Services Counselor
Oral Roberts University

Marc Kilmer
Independent Writer

Dale McLennan
Director, Career Center
Endicott College

ACKNOWLEDGMENTS
continued

Michael V Phillips
Career Development Counselor
University of North Carolina,
Wilmington

Alicia Sedberry
Assistant Director, Student & Alumni
Programs
University of Illinois, Chicago

Deborah Shields
Assistant Manager, Bainbridge Island Branch
Kitsap Credit Union

Justine Simon
Intern
Life After Graduation, LLC

N. Ross Thornburgh
Owner
Thornburgh Insurance Agency

I would also like to acknowledge and thank Kirrin Coleman for her interest, dedication, and support of this project. Your contributions to this guide far exceeded my expectations. In addition, I want to thank your husband, Morgan Coleman, and daughter, Sofie, for their patience and sacrifices during the development of this guide.

Finally, I want to thank my beautiful wife, Melissa, for her love and support. Without you, none of this would have been possible.

Terry Arndt
President
Life After Graduation, LLC

Table of Contents

Check Your Credit Report Now!
- Review it, repair it, & get on track
- Identity theft

Get a Grip on Your Finances

Live Within Your Means
- Find affordable housing
- Fake yourself out
- Eat in more often
- Be a "cheaper" date
- Shop smart

Read this Chapter Even Though It's About Insurance
- Health insurance
- Health care plans
- Flexible Spending Accounts (FSAs)
- Renter's insurance
- Auto insurance
- Insurance you don't need

Realistic Expectations

- The importance of having realistic expectations
- Employer needs/new employee needs
- Common causes of reality shock

Go Beyond Average

- Work a full day
- Do your job well
- Take the initiative
- Make the most of your mistakes
- Contribute positively to the organization
- Take care of yourself

What Your College Has to Offer You Now

- Networking
- Services

What You Have to Offer Your College

- Maintaining contact
- Mentoring
- Volunteer work
- Financial support

Introduction Congratulations, Graduate!

You are accomplished, educated, degreed, and ready to succeed in life. This transition period from student to professional can be both exhilarating and overwhelming. As your opportunities expand, so do the challenges. *Life After Graduation* will guide you through this process and help you achieve the success you desire.

You've mastered the art of student life: You can write a twenty-page paper in three hours, move all your belongings in an afternoon, and stretch your budget like Laffy Taffy. You've memorized the library hours, as well as every other study area on campus, and learned to eat cheaply at the local eateries. Of course, you also have knowledge of your subject area. You have skills. And chances are, you also have debt.

What you need now is a financial advisor, retirement planner, trusted insurance agent, career counselor, image consultant, marketing manager, and communications expert. And you need all the advice they have to offer as soon as possible. Well, look no further—we've done the legwork for you. We consulted experts in financial planning, insurance, and career development, then distilled everything they had to say about life after graduation into one little book. *Life After Graduation* covers all the relevant topics of this new phase of life—from what to expect of your first days on a new job to even planning for retirement.

In these chapters you'll find answers to all your important questions—including some you didn't even think to ask.

We'll address common questions like . . .

- What kind of insurance coverage do I need?

- How do I create a workable budget?

- Where can I find good—and inexpensive—financial and career advice?

- Why should I start investing in my retirement now?

- Should I consolidate my student loans?

- How can I make a great impression on my new boss and coworkers?

- What can I expect from my first few months on the job?

- How should I ask for a raise?

- How can I use my alumni connections to network?

Soon *you'll* be the expert on workplace culture and insurance riders and the best ways to trim variable expenses. In the meantime, ***Life After Graduation*** will be your go-to resource, your quick and complete guide to the essential terms and concepts you need to understand as you transition from student to professional.

Here's to your future!

Chapter 1

Check Your Credit Report Now!

You are what you owe, what you buy, and how timely you pay your bills. And all that other stuff that makes you who you are—personality, gestures, intelligence, wit—means nothing to credit card companies, student loan agencies, landlords, loan officers, and even some employers. What matters most to some is simply the content and quality of your credit report. And if they like what they see, you advance to the next step, whether that's another student loan, a cool apartment, or a new job.

So, why is everyone so interested in your credit report? What does it reveal about you? Think of it as a credit report card that provides a snapshot of your financial responsibility. First, it's a record of every time you apply for, or accept, a loan or other form of credit. Second, and most importantly, it tracks how you use your credit—how much you have available, how much you owe, and how you repay. The people who are considering hiring you, granting you a student loan, or giving you a new credit card simply want to know your financial track record.

Credit Report & Credit Score — What Are They?

Your entire financial credit history is compiled by one of several credit bureaus and then organized into the following formats:

- **Credit Report:** A detailed history of your borrowing habits for the past seven to ten years, your credit report is a record of what you owe and to whom, what you've paid, and if you've made any late payments. It also reveals personal information, such as your social security number, current and former addresses and telephone numbers. Any time you order a report or authorize someone else to do so, the inquiry is recorded.

- **Credit Score:** A credit score is a shorthand way for a lender to tell if you're a good credit risk or a bad one. A high score means you're lower risk and have a better chance of obtaining the best interest rates. While each credit bureau has its own system, they all take into account the following five factors: your ability to make payments on time, the amount of credit you owe, the type of credit you owe, the length of your credit history (the longer, the better), and the number of requests for new credit.

Who looks at my credit report?

Your landlord, employer, college, credit card company, bank, etc. all have an interest in reviewing your credit report.

Do *you* know what your credit report contains? How much do you owe? Do you have any late payment history? Worse, is someone else using your identity to rack up debt? Before you do anything else, you need to check your credit report and credit score.

Many people don't see their own credit report until they are about to make a major purchase—or unless they're mysteriously turned down at one of those retail shops that practically throws credit cards at customers. You need to be proactive with your credit. Check it and address any problems immediately.

GET YOUR FREE CREDIT REPORT NOW!!!
www.annualcreditreport.com
877-322-8228

The three major credit agencies are required by federal law to give consumers one FREE credit report per year. When you go to their websites, they will try to sell you a credit score as well as other services—don't worry about that stuff yet. Just get the free report.

By the way, the three major credit agencies are:

- **Equifax** (www.equifax.com)
- **Experian** (www.experian.com)
- **TransUnion** (www.transunion.com)

Conventional wisdom says that it takes years to remove a blemish from a credit report, but seconds to put one on. While that may be an exaggeration, you don't want to be in the position to find out. In fact, it's wise to contact each of the three major credit reporting firms—they have different methods of reporting, so you want to know what they all say about you—and request a credit report every four months. This will enable you to monitor and prevent any illegal use of your credit.

TIP

Order one free credit report every four months, rotating between the three major agencies. This is an inexpensive—*free!*—way to keep a close eye on your credit.

Ordering a credit report **DOES NOT** affect your credit score.

Applying for a credit card **DOES** affect your credit score.

Review it, repair it, & get on track

The first step to controlling your credit is to monitor it. The second step is to maintain and, if necessary, repair it. It's relatively easy

Pay that parking ticket!
(And return the library books while you're at it.)

Alma was stunned to discover that a long-forgotten parking ticket appeared on her credit report—and negatively impacted her score. "I had finally found the perfect car for the right price. When I went to the bank, though, I was told that my credit score was too poor to qualify me for the lower interest rate. A parking ticket—a measly $15 thing!—that I had gotten years before ended up costing me hundreds of dollars in higher car payments, not to mention the time and headache of getting that ticket off my record." As Alma discovered, many parking lot companies, libraries, and city governments do actively track (and report) people who don't pay fines.

to maintain and build your credit if you're starting with a strong foundation: Know what you owe, know who you owe, and pay your bills on time. If you move a lot, make sure every business you deal with has your change of address on file. Don't miss a payment because the vendor is sending bills to an old residence! Also, it's a good idea to set up a folder in your email account for e-bills, as they can easily get drowned in the inbox. Inadvertently missing a payment—even missing one because of the vendor's mistake—can cause as much headache as blatantly ignoring a due date.

Good To Know

Q: How can I develop a great credit history?

A: Building credit is simple:
- **Get credit**
- **Use it**
- **Pay it off**

While it's important to be cautious with your credit card use, don't make the mistake of not getting a credit card or never using the ones you have. Credit agencies want to see you have a history of good credit use.

Repairing your credit is more challenging than maintaining it, but it's definitely a project you should start as soon as possible. Even if you have a poor track record, you can eventually recover your credit.

Set up a system today for paying all current bills on time.

If you have big outstanding balances that you can't pay off, contact the businesses to see if they'll negotiate a payment plan with you.

Vendors would much rather have you pay them back directly than send your account to a collections agency which would not only ding your credit but cost the vendor big money in lost revenue.

Identity theft

Identity theft is a real problem and the best way to minimize your risk is to be on the offense. Why? Because you are a likely target: people aged 20 - 34 incur the highest rate of identity theft. And while it is a common problem, it is also a devastating one. On average it costs victims about $500 and takes an estimated 500 hours to clean up their credit report.

How can you prevent identity theft?

- Monitor your credit report and bank accounts.
- Keep a copy of all active credit cards and bank accounts so you can cancel them at a moment's notice.
- Control—as best you can—access to your personal information.

Where are you most vulnerable? Online, of course, and at the curb. Low tech identity thieves can do as much damage with unshredded bank statements and credit card offers they find in the trash as high tech thieves can do in cyberspace.

If you have been the victim of identity theft, contact your local consumer affairs office, your state attorney general's office, and the Federal Trade Commission (www.ftc.gov) right away. After you report the fraud, these agencies will give you step-by-step information on what to do to recover your credit.

TIP

Stop junk mail: Save the planet, and save yourself from identity theft.

You know those credit card offers that fill up your mailbox? "Act now!" "Lower your interest rate!" "Special offer!" Well, identity thieves know those offers, too. And if they get to your mailbox before you do—or rifle through your trash or recycling—they will have everything they need to co-opt your credit. Want to radically limit the number of credit card solicitations you receive in the mail—and greatly reduce your risk of identity theft?

After you order a credit report, call: (888) 5-OPT-OUT or visit www.ftc.gov

You can "opt out" of receiving junk mail. Once your name is on the national register, companies are legally bound to take your name off their mailing lists. (Note that you can choose to remain on the lists of certain companies or types of companies. So if you really want to keep getting those Victoria's Secret catalogues, just check the box that allows clothing retailers rights to your address.)

Chapter 2

Get a Grip on Your Finances

Now's the time to get a grip on your finances. First, a quick quiz: Which of the following statements best sums up your financial situation at the end of each month?

a) "Hmm…should I put this extra $1,100 into savings or invest it in something with a greater return?"

b) "Mmm…Toasty-O's for dinner! Again."

c) "Um…do you think the landlord will take Visa?"

d) "Ahh…nothing beats selling plasma on a sunny afternoon!"

If you answered A, you can probably get away with skimming this chapter. Most Americans, however, are not socking away $1,100 a month. Many of us are not putting *any* money at all into savings. In fact, the national savings rate is -.07%. That's right: *negative* point-oh-seven. So, while you might not be selling plasma in that last week before payday, chances are you could use a budget.

Budget. Like its cousin *diet*, the word *budget* is often used and rarely implemented. Both are the subject of countless conversations, articles, self-help books, and advertisements. Yet, curiously, we don't live in a nation of rich, thin people. Or even healthy, debt-free people.

Why the discrepancy? Well, everyone knows they *should* have a budget and *should* watch their diets, but many of us simply don't like *shoulds*. To many people, budgets and diets equal rules and restrictions: I *ought* to limit my spending, I *should* take the stairs instead of the elevator, I *can't* drink soda all day long. And we don't like rules. This is the land of rebellion, after all. This is the land of James Dean, leather jackets, and motorcycles.

But here's a secret, all you mavericks: A budget is your ticket to freedom. It's not really about restrictions and rules; it's about *you* deciding what to do and when to do it. And when you're in charge of your money—the earning, spending, and saving of it—you will be free.

So, how do you make a budget? It's easy to create and stick to a budget, but it's easier not to. Your first step, then, is to commit to the process, which means figuring out why you want and need a budget. Write down all of the reasons to create a budget and all of the reasons not to. Be honest with yourself and write down everything that comes to mind.

Consider This ...

Reasons to Budget	Reasons Not to Budget
I want to know where my money goes	It might cut into my clothes/clubbing/gambling/gear collecting habit
I work hard and want to keep more of the money I earn	I might miss the last-chance-only-happens-once-every-two-weeks sale
I want to buy a house	Retirement is for the weak!
I want to travel more	I'll have to live on thin gruel and watered-down coffee, I'll start wearing plastic bags instead of rain gear, I'll stop brushing my teeth, my girlfriend will break up with me...
I want an emergency fund	I'll become one of those weird people who opens their bank statements.
I want to retire by the time I'm....	People might think...

Three years out of college, Emily was not in control of her finances . . .

"I was making a pretty good salary, but I felt completely out of control of my finances. I was either oblivious or stressed about my money or both! The worst part is that when I felt stressed I went shopping, which didn't help matters." Finally, Emily sat down and got it all out on the table—literally. "First, I wrote down all of my debt. I had avoided dealing with it, but I realized that wasn't exactly helping me pay things off. Once it was in front of me I could begin to figure out how to get out of it. Looking at my financial situation straight on meant I could make concrete plans for my dreams, like owning my own home."

Once you've made the commitment, creating a budget is pretty easy (though expect it to take some time). Here are the four steps to budgeting:

1. Know your income. Quick! How much do you make before taxes? After taxes? How much do you contribute to savings or retirement? If you don't have answers to these three questions, get them. And if you do have an answer to that last question but it's something along the lines of "Savings? What savings?" or "It doesn't matter because retirement is for the old and I'm going to be young forever," then consider the following very carefully.

- You need to pay yourself first. Financial experts, life coaches, and investment gurus all advise you put at least 10% of your monthly gross income into savings or retirement right away—before you have a chance to spend it.

- The younger you are the more you should be thinking about retirement, because now is the time you can make a huge difference in when and how you retire. If, for example, you put $1,200 into an interest-bearing account right now, it will be worth about $25,000 by the time you retire. See Chapter 6 for details.

2. Track your spending. For at least one week, write down *every* expense. Carry around a little notepad and pen and jot down all purchases—every sandwich, pack of gum, tip, ATM fee, *every little thing*. To keep it simple, when you record the amounts, always round up.

If you space out and forget to note an expense, don't worry. Guesstimate the missing amount at the end of the day and write it down then.

Note: you might find it easier to carry around an envelope and collect receipts for every purchase you make throughout the day; then, in the evening, you can sit down and write them out. This method works just as well as the little-notebook-and-pen method, but be advised: the barista might look at you cockeyed if you ask him to write out a receipt for the 25-cent tip you plunked in his jar.

3. Find out where your money goes. The second step is to categorize and tally your monthly spending. The most common major categories are Housing, Food, Utilities, Debt, Insurance, Transportation, Entertainment, Personal, and Retirement/Savings. You will also want to create some subcategories in order to get a more precise picture of your spending patterns. For instance, Food should include the subcategories Groceries and Dining Out. Debt might include the subcategories Student Loan, Credit Cards, and Parents.

On a sheet of paper, or in a computer spreadsheet, write out your expense categories and subcategories, leaving adequate space under each heading to record your actual expenses. Now, using your bank statement, credit card statements, and the information you gathered while tracking your daily spending, categorize every expenditure. Remember to multiply the incidental expenses you tracked over the week by four, as now you're building a monthly record.

This information easily translates into your first **income statement**:

Monthly Income	$
Minus Monthly Fixed Expenses	– ($)
Minus Yearly Fixed Expenses (Monthly Average)	– ($)
Minus Monthly Variable Expenses	– ($)
Equals Remaining Income	= $

Once you have a picture of how you earn, save, and spend your money, decide what you want to do about it in the future. Then put your plan into writing to ensure you'll stick to it.

4. Fix the leaks! Is your money leaking away, deflating your wallet along with your future spending and saving choices?

As you review your spending leaks, it will probably become obvious what you need to do to fix them. The trick is to do just that and to do it as soon as possible so you can avoid letting your hard-earned money dribble away.

Here are some quick fixes once you recognize the leaks:

- **Pay attention.** Know what you're spending, when you're spending it, and why you're spending it. Also, pay attention to the rates you're paying for credit card interest, services, and other variable expenses. If you're regularly stuck with a late payment charge on a bill, write a reminder on the calendar or just pay the bill the day it comes in the mail.
- **Take stock of all the expenses in your life, no matter how minor.** Do you use the online photo membership that pulls $4.95 from your account automatically every month?

Do you need that subscription to the newspaper or could you get your news online? Do you regularly go to the gas station that charges .05 more per gallon because the cheaper one is on the other side of the street? Little changes can make a big impact. Even if these quick fixes won't make you an instant millionaire, isn't it nice to know that you'll end up with more of your money than the executives at the cell phone company?

TIP

Common Money Leaks

- Daily nonessentials (see "The Real Cost of that Latte")

- Fees (most common: using another bank's ATM, late fees for bills)

- High-interest credit cards

- Unused memberships, services, and subscriptions

- Convenience items

- **Consider the real price of convenience.** You're a busy person. But convenience spending might mean that you're working double time for the benefit of the drycleaner, the take-out teriyaki shop, and the parking garage owner. Sure, it might save you five minutes to use the other bank's ATM, but you can save $2.50— and get some exercise—if you walk a block to your own bank.

Now you know the ins and outs of budgeting and are as prepared as

The Real Cost of That Latte
(or Soda, or Bottled Water, or Pack of Gum...)

Consider This ...

What would you do if you won $1,000 on the local radio station giveaway? Shriek? Pump your fist in the air? Well, get ready to jump up and down on the sofa, because you're about to win $1,000 or more!

Look at your little daily nonessential expenses. A latte here, a smoothie there, a pack of gum, the latest issue of *Time* magazine... If you cut this spending by just $3 a day, you will save $1,095 in a year, $5,475 in 5 years, and over $20,000 in 20 years! Now, if you go beyond saving and invest that $3 a day, the numbers look even better (and the latte looks even less appealing). At a conservative rate of return, you'd have over $26,000 in 15 years and a whopping $43,650 in 20 years.

You already have the money, now you need to keep more of it. (Feel free to shriek and pump your fist in the air the next time you pass that cool, jazz-infused, well-lit coffee shop without spending your money there.)

anybody to manage your money wisely. However, there's one more thing to keep in mind as you begin the process: The way you think about and deal with money is ultimately a habit. And as with any other habit, altering your approach to your personal finances may entail trials and backslides. If mantras like "Don't ask, don't tell" or "Spend it when you got it" have guided your spending habits for years, they will continue to do so unless you make a conscious decision to change your behavior. Think up some new mantras— how about "Keep it 'cause you earn it" or "Early retirement beats name brand"?—and revisit this chapter often to help you *keep* a grip on your finances.

Chapter 3

Live Within Your Means

The quick version of this chapter goes something like this: Move back in with your folks. Shop less. Eat in. Save more. Easy enough, you say, but what to wear? The answer is, "neutrals."

We all pretty much know the basics of how to live cheaply, so why is it so hard to suck it up for a few years, then revel in accumulated wealth in the not-so-distant future? The problem is that conventional wisdom is often drowned out by the siren song of popular culture, advertising, and easy credit: "Here it is! You want it? You got it!" After all, without these forces, who would have guessed that people look so cute with little dogs? Or that little dogs look so cute in rhinestone-studded collars, snugged up in pink fluffy beds, gnawing on teeny organic doggie biscuits? Or that the whole package—dog, collar, bed, biscuits—can be purchased now and paid for later? Unfortunately, celebrities— who can easily afford the whole shebang, make it look not just easy but necessary.

Now, most of us aren't so easily swayed that we'll go out and buy a Maltese just because our favorite rock star has one. But the twin influences of media and easy access to "money" have undeniably put their stamp on our culture.

"I want" becomes "I need" becomes "I need it now." Resist the siren song and you'll be miles ahead of the pack, enjoying leisure time while some poor soul is working to pay off ten-year-old credit card bills.

The future beckons, but for now here's how to make the most of the present.

Find affordable housing

The first step to living within your means is to find inexpensive housing. A bachelor pad in downtown Seattle—or San Francisco or Atlanta or Chicago—is perfect for entertaining new friends and decorating with sleek laminate furniture from Sweden. However, such a lifestyle can eat up your earnings faster than you can say, "Let's go back to my place and look at the skyline." Housing takes a 25% bite out of most people's income, and even more if they live alone in a metropolitan area.

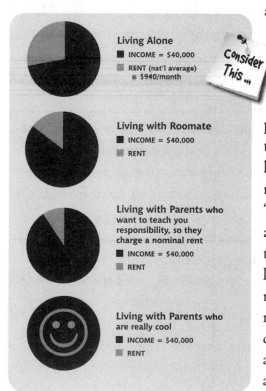

Living Alone
■ INCOME = $40,000
▨ RENT (nat'l average) = $940/month

Consider This ...

Living with Roomate
■ INCOME = $40,000
▨ RENT

Living with Parents who want to teach you responsibility, so they charge a nominal rent
■ INCOME = $40,000
▨ RENT

Living with Parents who are really cool
■ INCOME = $40,000
▨ RENT

Have you checked out central Wyoming lately? How about that recently-converted rec room in your parents' house? OK, OK, if those options are unrealistic, how about seriously reconsidering your oath to "Never have a roommate again as long as I live!" Sure, there are limitations to living back at home or with roommates, but think how much money you'll save! You could pay down debts, invest, and build a real savings account.

Fake yourself out

live like you're poor (or poorer than you are) and you'll get rich; Live like you're rich (or richer than you are) and you'll get poor. In other words, live below your means. You can fake yourself out by directing, as most financial experts suggest, 10% of your gross income into savings and investments (or paying off debt) before you even lay eyes on it. Pay yourself first. (See Chapter 2.)

Bring Back Cash!

Cash seems almost quaint these days, little green bills with pictures of old men on them, little jingly coins that go in those funny phones in the glass booths. But maybe it's time to go retro. Study after study has shown that when you pay with cash you spend less; when you pay with debit or credit, you spend more. *The Wall Street Journal* reported that card companies see the average transaction at McDonald's jump from $4.50 to $7 when customers use debit or credit instead of cash. It's the difference between spending money and spending "money."

To Do!

Eat in more often

Food is usually about 13% of a person's income, but it's a variable expense so a great place to "tighten the belt." The best ways to trim your food budget:

- **Eat at home.** If eating is a big part of your social scene, do more dinners at home with friends.
- **Avoid appetizers and drinks.** Remember that waiters love it when you order drinks, desserts, and appetizers. Avoid these extras: They usually have the biggest profit margins and really pad your bill. (For the price of one soda, you can buy six at the grocery store.)
- **Buy store brands.** Often, store brands are manufactured by the same folks who make the name-brand stuff. Even when they're not, the substantial savings you get with the store-brand products will make you forget any taste difference.
- **Buy in bulk.** Sometimes. If it makes sense for your lifestyle. Do you drink gallons of coffee a week? Then buy it in bulk. One caution about the mega-warehouse-super stores: It's easy

to get distracted and talk yourself into overbuying because it's such a good deal.

- **Shop at the Farmers Market.** The prices are often less than grocery stores and the produce is fresh!

Be a "cheaper" date

There's lots of fun to be had for very little money. Check your local newspaper for bargain movies, eats, and other date ideas. Also, check out city guides from your library. They often include lesser known (and cheap) entertainment options. Two habits to nix if you have them: 1) Going shopping at the mall for entertainment and, 2) Buying rounds of drinks.

Consider This ...

Cheap Date Ideas

- Check out the local music scene.
- Attend a seasonal festival or street fair.
- Go for a walk (cliché, but never underestimate the power of a walk on the beach at sunset).
- Try Chinese, Vietnamese, Korean, West African, Cuban food — a lot of the best restaurants have lower ticket prices than the usual pub grub.
- Visit a museum.
- Picnic (or BBQ) in the park.
- Keep your eye out for community events, such as monthly art walks, weekly outdoor movies, or other fun and inexpensive ways to experience local nightlife.

Shop smart

Because clothing generally accounts for 5% of a person's budget, it's worth including here. It is a variable expense that some of us find hard to control. Here's how to keep your clothing appetite in check:

- **Buy clothes at the very end or very beginning of the season.** The $300 jacket you saw in October was $130 in August and will be $120 in December.

- **Shop for staples**—t-shirts, underwear, socks—at one of the giant retail stores, like Target and Wal-Mart.

- **Fill your wardrobe with black and neutrals.** This will allow you to mix and match most of your outfits and they'll all look fresh and chic.

- **Shop second hand.** It's an easy way to be creative on a budget. Plus, you can find some trendy pieces at thrift stores and consignment shops.

So that's it: the quick and the not-so-quick versions of how to live cheaply. If you want to get truly frugal you can visit websites dedicated to really stretching dollars (Create rubber bands by cutting up used latex gloves! Make wrapping paper out of old junk mail!). However, you don't necessarily need to radically alter your lifestyle in order to keep more money and spend less. Make a few adjustments at a time and pretty soon you'll be so distracted by your swelling bank account that you won't notice you're picking up dates in your parents' minivan.

Four Easy Non-Spending Habits

- **Ask Yourself,** "Is this necessary?" By asking yourself if you really need something, you will be forced to pay attention to what you're spending and why.

- **Say No to Add-Ons.** Extra insurance, the "deluxe" car wash, dessert...there are innumerable opportunities to "super size" your expenses. Recognize and avoid them.

- **Spend Nothing Day.** Designate one day a week—or a month—a "Spend Nothing Day." Not only will you save money on the designated day, but it will help you see how much and how frequently you spend on the other days.

- **Cool Down.** Give yourself at least 24 hours to think about any purchases over $100. Also, take an item back if you get home and realize it isn't something you really, really want or need.

Chapter 4

Read this Chapter
Even Though It's About Insurance

Insurance is like a GPS unit. When hiking and conditions are good, you don't have to think about it and when conditions are bad, you're glad you brought it along. Plus it looks gadgety and cool. Scratch that. Insurance has, in fact, nothing to do with anything that is fun or remotely cool. Insurance at its best is dull…until you have to make a claim. Then it's absolutely necessary.

Even if you're broke, young, healthy, and cool? Yes, you still need insurance, but the difference between you and those of us who write this kind of advice is that when *you* write out the checks to the insurance company, you can console yourself by saying, "At least I'm still young, healthy and cool!" And that's worth something.

But let's address the other part of the above scenario—the writing-the-check-out part. It's not pleasant to pay for insurance, no matter your age or financial status. When all goes well, after all, you don't need it. It's understandable that some people see insurance payments as self-imposed hardship or proof of having been suckered into some silly deal. But, the truth is that you are definitely not a sucker.

As a recent college graduate, you probably need four or five types of insurance. These include:

- Auto Insurance
- Health Insurance
- Life Insurance
- Home Owner's/Renter's Insurance
- Disability Insurance

Zero to sixty in eight seconds.

Ian G. was 23 with $380 of debt when his car hit a piece of debris and careened off the highway. Luckily, he has no long-term injuries from the accident, but because he had no auto or health insurance, he still lives with the financial burden—over $60,000 in medical fees.

You are, in fact, a well-informed (if slightly broke) consumer—who can find appropriate, affordable insurance coverage. The real hardship, however, comes from not having the right insurance coverage when you need it. Read on to find out more.

Health insurance

This is a must. Even if you are young and healthy, it is an enormous risk to go without health coverage. Taking such a risk—even for a few months—could have devastating consequences. The out-of-pocket cost of a broken ankle is over $1,500.

Going to the ER for a sore throat, getting tested, and being told to go home and get some rest will run you about $500. (Of course, avoiding the ER when you *do* have a serious illness can cost even more.) And these examples are small potatoes next to catastrophic illnesses, which can easily rack up tens and even hundreds of thousands of dollars.

Despite these alarming facts, many recent graduates are inclined to take a gamble and go without health insurance. In fact, 18- to 24-year-olds are the least likely of any age group to have health insurance: Over 30% of people in this age bracket are uninsured. There are several reasons for this statistic. Up to age 18, most people are insured under their parents' policy. However, such eligibility stops (depending on the insurance plan) anywhere from age 18 to age 24. Many college students rely on their parents' policy for as long as possible, then switch to their university plan, which is relatively inexpensive.

As they make the next transition—from college to the working world—they suddenly face a gap in coverage that may seem too expensive or too trivial to fix.

While this is an understandable response when you're young, healthy and broke, it's important to understand that stuff happens and it tends to happen when it's least convenient or foreseeable. Even if you're employed right out of college, it may take a few months before your employer's coverage kicks in. Here are some options to help you bridge the gap and stay insured:

COBRA: The Consolidated Omnibus Budget Reconciliation Act guarantees that workers can maintain their health insurance when they leave a job, but it also applies to college students. If you've been covered under your parents' policy, you can keep that coverage for up to 18 months— if you pay the premiums. Not cheap, but it keeps you covered. Note: you typically have just 60 days after graduation to apply.

> **Key Vocabulary: A Quick Primer on Insurance Terms**
>
> GOOD TO KNOW
>
> **Premium:** The fee you pay, usually assessed annually or semiannually
>
> **Deductible:** The amount of money you have to pay on a claim before the insurance kicks in. A higher deductible means a lower premium.
>
> **Rider:** A provision attached to a policy that adds to or changes the original policy.

University Health Plan: If you have been participating in your college's health care plan, you can extend this coverage as well. You'll get to keep your doctors, but you will have to pay higher premiums and the coverage usually only lasts a few months. Other possible resources for inexpensive health plans include your alumni office, fraternity/sorority, or other college affiliate.

Short-Term Policy: Cheaper than the other options—and higher risk—these policies generally cover one to six months. Designed to cover unexpected events, but don't usually cover preventative healthcare or pre-existing conditions. Check with your Alumni Association as they often have short term policies available.

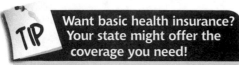

TIP

Want basic health insurance? Your state might offer the coverage you need!

Georgetown University Health Policy Institute manages a great website that offers a complete, state-by-state guide to health insurance: **www.healthinsuranceinfo.net**

Major Medical Policy: The name says a lot. This bare-bones coverage generally pays for hospital stays. Not doctors' fees, but the cost of room and food while you're hospitalized.

Health Savings Account (HSA): More and more people are investing in tax-advantaged Health Savings Accounts to provide for their medical expenses. Health Savings Accounts allow you or your employer to contribute pre-tax dollars into a designated account for medical expenses. The money is only taxed if you withdraw it for non-medical purposes. You must be enrolled in a High Deductible Health Plan to qualify for a HSA.

Health insurance is expensive, but not having it can be financially devastating. Choose a plan that makes sense for your lifestyle. A short-term policy might work very well for someone who is in excellent health and needs coverage for just a couple of months; however, someone who has a family or personal history of illness or who foresees a longer gap in coverage should probably opt to pay more in order to get good preventative care.

Health care plans

It used to be that if you got sick you could just send your brother for a doctor. He would ride for four days across the frozen plain to bring the local doctor right to your bedside. Sure, there might be leeches and bloodletting involved, but you'd get personalized service and you could pay for it with eggs, pickles, and cords of wood! By comparison, health care today is sterile and complicated. (However, life expectancy is up by a few decades, so there's a trade-off.)

The **fee-for-service insurance plan** most closely resembles the personalized service of the days of yore (minus the bloodletting, of course). With this type of plan, you can choose any doctor and any hospital you want, and the insurance company pays between 80 to 100 percent of the expense. What's the catch? Fee-for-service plans are generally *very* expensive.

Most people now are covered by managed-care plans instead. Here are descriptions of the most common managed-care health insurance models:

Health Maintenance Organizations (HMOs): HMOs provide health care through a network of doctors, hospitals, and medical professionals. Participants and/or their employers pay a monthly premium in exchange for the HMO's comprehensive care. Participants must seek care from network primary care physicians (PCPs) and must have a PCP referral in order to see a specialist.

Preferred Provider Organizations (PPOs): PPOs have a network of preferred healthcare providers, but participants may elect to seek care from a physician outside the network if they are willing to pay more. Unlike HMOs, PPOs generally allow participants to access specialists without a referral.

Hybrid, or Point-Of-Service (POS) Plans: POSs allow participants to see providers outside the preferred provider network (like PPOs) for a slightly higher co-payment or deductible, but they require participants to select a primary care physician (like HMOs).

At a Glance: Compare Health Insurance Plans

Good To Know

	Overall Flexibility	Overall Cost	Choice of Physician	Easy Access to Specialists	Premiums	Deductibles	Co-Payments	Out-of-Pocket expenses	Paperwork (reimbursement forms)
HMO	Low	Low	Within network only	Need referral	Low	None	Low	Low	Low
POS (Hybrid)	Moderate	Low - Moderate	Within network encouraged	Need referral	Low-Moderate	None	Low (except for non-network care)	Low	Moderate
PPO	Moderate-High	Moderate-High	Within network encouraged	Yes	Moderate-high	Moderate	Vary	Moderate-High	High
Fee-For-Service	High	High	Yes	Yes	High	High	N/A	High	High

Flexible Spending Accounts (FSAs)

Finally! An acronym that can save you some money! An FSA lets you pay for your health care over the course of the year—with before-tax dollars. This lowers your taxable salary and can save you over $1,000 a year.

First, estimate how much you'll spend in a year on health care—consider the cost of co-payments, aspirin, bandages, cold medicines, prescriptions, etc. Next, through your employer and an FSA coordinator, contribute a portion of your paycheck to your FSA. Finally, document and report health-related expenses to the FSA, which will reimburse you. As you can see, it's not a difficult process but it might be confusing. Remember to estimate your expenses carefully at the beginning of the year; any contributions left over in your account at the end of the year vanish—FSA accounts do *not* carry over from year to year. Also, hold on to all those receipts and other documentation of health care expenses, as you'll need to itemize them in order to get full reimbursement.

Renter's insurance

While health insurance involves endless terms, acronyms, what-ifs, and a not insignificant portion of your salary, renter's insurance is simple: Protect your stuff for cheap. You can get a good policy for as low as $100 a year. A paltry fee for a lot of peace of mind.

What's covered? Damage to or loss of your computer, MP3 player, other electronics, sports equipment, clothing, and furniture. (Remember: If your apartment is burgled or burned or mold-infested, your landlord is not responsible for your stuff.) These policies even cover your belongings when you're in transition (moving across country, for instance). And if you have irreplaceable objects—jewelry, original artwork, antiques, LPs—you can pay a little more and add a rider for them to your policy.

Another important aspect to renter's insurance is liability coverage. If someone falls and hurts himself at your place, if an appliance overheats and starts a fire, or if your cute Maltese bites a visitor— well, you might be covered if you get sued.

Auto insurance

If you have a car, you must have auto insurance. "Must," as in "are legally required to," at least in most places. Almost all states require car owners to have automobile liability insurance. Despite these laws, there are plenty of uninsured drivers anyway, which is another reason for *you* to have complete coverage. Insurance, after all, is really about your financial protection. An auto accident can wipe out the uninsured beyond physical and emotional damage, leaving a person vulnerable to lawsuits and staggering hospital bills.

The following are major categories of automobile insurance. The first four are highly recommended and/or legally required, depending on your state:

Bodily Injury Liability: If you injure someone, this component of your insurance covers the injured party's medical costs. Most states require that motorists have some bodily injury coverage. Your insurance agent can tell you what that minimum is. It's also a good idea to increase your coverage in this area as your assets grow; the more you have the more you can be sued for and the more liability coverage you need.

Property Damage Liability: This covers the costs to repair or replace damaged property—other vehicles, roadway signs and structures, buildings, etc. This is not always a legal responsibility, but it's an important aspect to financial protection.

Medical Payments or Personal Injury Protection (PIP): This covers medical expenses of the driver and passengers, regardless of who is at fault. It also covers injuries you may suffer when riding in or driving another person's car.

Uninsured/Underinsured Motorist Liability: An estimated 14% of drivers on the road do not have insurance or have inadequate coverage. So if one of them slams into your car, you need to have some way of paying for repairs to you and the car. This component of your auto insurance will cover lost wages, medical expenses, and property damage resulting from a run-in with an uninsured motorist.

The following categories are not necessary for every driver. If you drive a junker with missing floorboards, mushrooms in the upholstery, and a "Vote for Nixon" bumper sticker, you can probably forego collision and comprehensive coverage. However, if you're still making payments, your lender might require these.

Collision: Covers damage to your car caused by an automobile accident, whether or not you are at fault.

Comprehensive (Fire and Theft): Covers non-collision damage, such as vandalism, hail dents, and tree damage.

One common question related to auto insurance is, "Do I need to purchase insurance when I rent a car?"

GOOD TO KNOW

Love the Blue Book, Hate the Blue Book. Type in "blue book" on your favorite search engine and you'll come up with sites that contain charts of the fair market value of automobiles (Kelley Blue Book and Nada Guides are two such guides). You'll love knowing the fair market value when you're purchasing a used car, as that magic number can give you the leverage you need to talk a salesperson down in price. However, when it comes to insurance, the blue book value can leave you feeling a little deflated. A car you absolutely love—maybe a first car, one you've driven cross country, one that's seen you through great dates and break-ups, one you've even *named*—well, according to the blue book it's worth $390. And that's the amount of the check from the insurance company that will "cover" the loss of the car if it's totaled. Sigh.

The answer is maybe. If your own insurance policy does not have collision or comprehensive, then you should accept the rental agency's plan. If your policy does include collision or comprehensive, it should cover you when you're driving a rental, but it's always a good idea to double check with them before you're standing at the rental car company counter. Also, if you are paying for the rental car with a credit card, check with your credit card company about coverage. Many credit card providers offer Collision Damage Waiver coverage as a benefit to card holders.

Tips for Controlling the Cost of Auto Insurance

1. **Compare prices and coverage,** but remember that cheaper can cost you more in the long run. You want to know if you can afford the premiums and what kind of service and coverage you'll actually get if you end up in an accident. Check the Better Business Bureau (www.bbb.org) to learn more about a company's track record.

2. **Remember: Premium up, deductible down.** Deductible up, premium down. If your finances could weather a higher deductible, you probably want to opt for a lower premium.

3. **Calculate the cost of insurance before you buy a car.** Some cars cost more to insure, either because they're simply more expensive, or speedier, or more likely to get jacked.

4. **Drive less, pay less.** Your mileage is included in insurance calculations, so if you choose public transportation for commuting rather than your car, you'll pay less for coverage.

5. **Keep your record clean.** Of course, DUIs, DWIs, and other traffic violations will raise your rates considerably.

6. **Learn how to lower your insurance.** If you have airbags, park in a garage, have an alarm, and take a defensive driving course, for instance, you could find yourself with a very pleasing premium. Also ask about discounts if you consolidate all your insurance needs with one provider.

7. **Talk to your parents' provider.** If you have been covered under their policy, their insurance company has a record of your driving record and claims. If you have a clean record, they can often provide discounts other providers cannot.

Insurance you don't need

You've heard a lot about what you must have, should have, need to get. Now we're going to tell you what you might not need and definitely don't want. Insurance is for stuff that matters—your health and your financial well-being. It is not for little stuff, like MP3 players or TVs. Here's a short list of what you can probably pass on:

Extended Warranty and Repair Plans: The nice man with the polo shirt has spent a lot of time convincing you whatever he's selling is a great product. Well, then, it doesn't need "insurance." Say no. Even if it breaks, you'll come out ahead.

Home Warranty Plans: Accept a home warranty if it's already part of the selling package, but don't pay to tack one on. Hire a really thorough home inspector with the money you save to make sure the house you're buying is sound.

Credit Life and Credit Disability Policies: These show up as offers in your bank and credit card statements. They are fairly inexpensive, but the corresponding benefits are low, too. If you have life insurance or disability insurance, these credit policies are especially redundant.

Your individual insurance needs depend on a variety of factors. Before you set out to purchase insurance, arm yourself with knowledge: Read up, check with other sources, and know what you want to get into. The more you know, the better coverage you'll have and the more money you'll save.

Chapter 5

Plan for Emergencies

Worst-case scenarios don't make great dinner conversation. "Think about it: you could get fired, just like that, and be out of work for, like, months! And have you given much thought to flesh-eating bacteria? Did you know you could get it from the teeniest little cut? Sometimes I just think about how much it would suck to get into a really bad car accident. Do you ever wonder about that? Pass the salsa, will you?" In fact, a lot of us, when someone brings up the unthinkable, do the equivalent of a child's response to something she doesn't want to hear: We plug our ears and sing, "La! La! Not listening! Not listening!"

We don't have to get morbid here, but it's worth unplugging the ears for a minute to acknowledge that, yes, bad stuff happens. Accidents, medical emergencies, unexpected unemployment—they are unpredictable, sometimes frightening, and definitely part of every person's life. We don't know everything that we'll

Did you know?

Consider This ...

The average length of unemployment in the United States is over *four months!*

face in our lives, but we can prepare financially so that if and when something happens, we'll be as ready as possible.

Everybody needs some kind of emergency fund that can cover their expenses for a while if they find themselves incapacitated, unemployed, or simply faced with a knock-out expense. Nobody expects the busted transmission or Sunday morning plumbing emergency. People without the means to keep themselves financially afloat after disaster strikes often find themselves awash in credit card debt.

Do you know how expensive a root canal at 18% interest is? Let's just say that at least in the dentist's chair you get painkillers. When you're home three years later writing out another check to your credit card company—now, *that's* pain. How much you need in your fund, how you'll build it, and where you'll keep it is what this chapter will help you figure out.

How in the heck can I create an emergency fund when I'm so broke I have to order pizza with 2 toppings instead of 3?

If you've got your budget figured out so closely that you know the number of toppings you can afford, kudos! Now, have you thought about ordering plain pizza and adding your own toppings? Kidding. Kind of.

Like most people at your stage of life, you might not be able to afford to contribute a lot right now. However, it is important to make your future self a priority. You *can* begin an emergency fund and we have some tips on how to trick yourself into paying into it without feeling more strapped.

How much should I keep in my emergency fund?

Financial experts agree that you should have such a fund, but they disagree as to how much you need in it. Most experts, though, say that a person should have between two to six months of their minimum monthly living expenses socked away. At your stage of life it's appropriate to work toward the low end of the spectrum: Aim for building a reserve worth at least two to three months of your minimum living expenses.

How can I build an emergency fund?

Once you figure out how much you need, you can create a monthly payment schedule for yourself. Calculate your projected total, then break that into manageable monthly payments. On the first of every month, for instance, write a $100 check to your emergency account. (Or better yet, arrange to have it automatically transferred.) People are much more likely to contribute consistently to a savings or retirement account if they do it as soon as—or even before—their paycheck hits their checking account. You really won't notice these deductions.

Sample Emergency Fund Plan

To figure out how much you need to sock away, add up your minimum monthly expenses. Only include real necessities.

Rent	$850
Food	$250
Health Insurance	$200
Utilities	$80
Transportation	$95
Monthly Total	$1,475
Emergency Fund (for 3 months)	$4,425

At $100 a month, it will take you about three and a half years to create a $4,000 reserve. Sure, it's the tortoise approach, but you need to sustain the contribution rate. Pace yourself. If you're certain you can contribute more, however, go for it. If you've looked over your budget and can only afford $50, do it. Some is better than none. In fact, put a little sum in an account *right now*, then you can read the rest of this chapter knowing you've got a head start.

The "Shove It!" Fund

Mary Jean R., of Asheville, North Carolina, recounts this piece of motherly advice: "When I graduated from college, my mom handed me an envelope. It contained a money market statement—in my name—from a bank I had never even stepped foot in. The balance showed $100. 'It's your 'Shove It!' money,' Mom said. 'Put $50 into it every month. In a while you'll have enough in there to know that you can survive a little unemployment.' She wanted me never to feel trapped in an intolerable job. I've never had to crack into that account and I think that's partly because I know it's there—when I've had a rough day at work or a particularly unreasonable boss, I think to myself, 'Well, I could tell them to shove it.' It makes me feel powerful. I'm turning 30 this month and I have over $7,000 in that little bank."

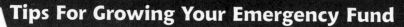

Tips For Growing Your Emergency Fund

TIP

Adopt a couple of these habits and you'll be surprised at how quickly your reserve grows (and how little you notice your contributions).

1. **Coin jar.** Treat coins as decorative objects rather than currency; never use them to actually pay for anything. Up the ante by using cash frequently (instead of your debit card), which will give you even more opportunities to feed that coin jar.

2. **Halve your gift money.** Does grandma still send you birthday checks? Imagine her delight when your thank-you card tells her how much you enjoyed spending half on a little birthday treat for yourself and depositing half into savings! There's more than one way to treat yourself, after all.

3. **Get physical.** Tie a monetary reward to another personal goal. For instance, if you've resolved to work out four times a week, make a "tip jar" that you can feed every time you actually do work out. Add $1 each time and you'll be able to see your progress toward both goals—by the end of the year you'll have over $200 and rock hard glutes.

4. **Break a habit to make a habit.** Do you have a frivolous expense habit? Something that you purchase on a regular basis that leaks money? Take a break from the habit and put the difference you save into your emergency fund. Instead of purchasing a new paperback, check it out at the library. Ka-ching! You can deposit $12.99. Go from eating out four times a week to two. You'll save money by eating at home, and you can deposit the rest.

5. **Keep paying retired bills.** Did you pay your car off? Awesome. If you're used to a $250 per month expense like a car payment, you can keep it up—but this time give it to yourself. Same goes for utility bills, which often vary seasonally. If your electric bill is high in the winter and low in the summer, you can budget for the high bills and pay yourself the difference in those warmer months.

6. **Tax refund.** Chances are pretty good that you will receive a tax refund the first couple years after graduation. Avoid the temptation to spend it. Instead, make a nice contribution to your emergency fund.

Where should I keep my emergency fund?

That's a really good question. There are two general rules about placing your emergency money:

1) You need to be able to access the funds quickly, but not too quickly.

Do choose a bank and type of account that makes it easy for you to deposit funds on a regular basis. *Do not* put these funds into your regular savings account, especially if it's linked to your checking account. That will make it too easy for you to tap into if you have an "emergency" urge to buy a great pair of shoes or need an "emergency" night out on the town. Some people set up accounts in a bank across town or one that doesn't have a lot of ATMs available, just so they can reduce access (and temptation). Also, it's not a good idea to put your emergency funds into stocks, as they're higher risk and usually harder to cash out.

Emergency Fund Accounts

Good To Know

Here are the questions to ask when searching for the right place for your emergency money:

- Is the account FDIC insured?
- How much interest will it earn?
- Does it require a minimum opening amount?
- Does it require a minimum balance?
- Does your money need to be in the account for a certain amount of time?
- Are there any fees associated with the account?

Note that one account might be best when you're starting out, but another will be a better choice in a year, as you accrue more money. You might begin by putting money into a high-interest savings account because you can access it quickly. After twelve months, you can transfer it to a long-term CD that earns even more interest, and build up the savings account again.

2) Your money should be earning interest (let it work while you work).

If you keep it in your coin jar or under your mattress, your money will just lose value. Inflation in the past decade has hovered around 3%. That means that $1,000 tucked under a mattress will be worth only about $970 in a year. You want your hard-earned money to keep up with—or, preferably, outpace—inflation. **Note:** many savings accounts do not offer a return higher than the rate of inflation. Check out high-interest savings accounts, money market accounts (MMAs), certificates of deposits (CDs), and bonds.

There are enough unpredictables in life—but your finances are, to a very large extent, within your control. The truth is that imagining worst-case scenarios may not be great dinner conversation. But, if doing so helps you establish financial priorities and put those priorities into action, you will ultimately reduce anxiety in your life.

Chapter 6

Got Retirement?

This topic is pretty important, so it's fitting here to turn to ancient wisdom. More specifically, to the ancient wisdom of Lao Tzu, who said in his great text *The Way of Lao Tzu*, "A journey of a thousand miles begins with a single step." Now, Lao Tzu died when he was 35, so we'll never know what he would have said about compounding interest and Roth IRAs, but one can speculate he'd have this advice about retirement in general: "Start that thing now, baby!"

To which you might understandably reply, "But, Lao Tzu, sir, teacher, I am young and poor and retirement is a distant land for old people who wear wrinkle-free pants and talk about fiber all the time. What have I to do with that?" To which he might (understandably) shake his head and pull out a chart that looks something like this:

Think about this for a second: Invest $1,000 when you're 25 and it will grow (this chart assumes your money earns a conservative 8% interest) to $21,725 by the time you're 65!

Now, wait five years and invest the $1,000 when you're 30 and your money still grows, but at age 65 you'll have $14,785, quite a chunk of change for a $1,000 investment, but substantially less than if you had invested it when you were younger.

And that's the key: You are young now. The best time to invest in your retirement is now. You may or may not have much money to put aside for retirement, but you have time. Compound interest will make even a modest monthly investment a substantial retirement fund. Imagine yourself thirty-five or forty years now (or even fifteen years from now, if you're really serious about preparing for an early retirement): What would you say to your younger, just-graduated-from-college self?

Would you regret contributing to a retirement account? Would you regret not contributing to one?

Who Will Pay for Your Retirement?

GOOD TO KNOW

You. If you want a comfortable, worry-free retirement it's up to you, and you alone. Your grandparents' generation had pensions and Social Security and, because of shorter life expectancy, fewer post-working years to provide for. The likelihood that you'll work for a company that offers a pension is very small, that you'll work for that company long enough to earn a worthwhile pension practically nonexistent. Social Security? You'll keep paying into it, but don't expect to get much out of it. Very few retirees *today* find it an adequate sole income. Whatever you get from Uncle Sam should be considered a bonus, absolutely not the basis of your retirement.

The destination is an enjoyable, fruitful, anxiety-free retirement and, whether yours will be one of wrinkle-free pants or short shorts, the single step that begins the journey is investing in a retirement account. The earlier, the better.

How much money do you need to retire?

The answer to this question is: A lot. What "a lot" means depends on what retirement means to you. Do you want a kayak, Bayliner, or yacht? Do you see yourself taking walks, golfing, or heli-skiing? Think about how young you want to be when you retire, what kind of lifestyle you hope to have in retirement, and calculate from there. Many financial experts recommend you aim for 75% of your annual salary, based on your last few years of employment, available for each year of retirement. This might be a working figure for you, especially if your housing costs will be limited by then (if, for example, you've paid off your mortgage by the time you retire). Of course, other variables come into play: What will a dollar be worth when you retire? How much will inflation eat up your retirement earnings? How much will you be paying for health care when you reach that age? You can find many online retirement calculators that can help you get started figuring out how much you'll need in order to retire comfortably. (A good basic retirement calculator awaits at www.aarp.org.)

Retirement plan options

There are two broad categories of retirement plans: defined benefit plans and employer-sponsored plans. (We'll cover plans for the self-employed in the next section.)

Defined benefit plans are commonly referred to as pension plans, and they used to be the standard: You graduate, find employment with Company Bluechip, work there for 30 years, retire, and Company Bluechip pays you a monthly pension based on a calculation of your years of service and salary. "Defined benefit" is a promise: In exchange for your hard work and loyalty, we will invest on behalf of you and your coworkers, and continue to provide for you in your retirement years.

These plans are not as common now as they were in your grandparents' generation. Why not? They are expensive for companies to maintain (partly because of those pesky increases in life expectancy!); companies can no longer expect, and employees no longer promise, long-term loyalty; and the workforce has exerted pressure—especially in bull markets—to command its own investments. Hence, the emphasis now is on employer-sponsored plans.

Employer-sponsored plans, also known as defined-contribution plans, include the 401 (k), 403 (b) and 457. (To limit some clunkiness, we'll refer to all these related plans as 401(k).) These plans do not guarantee a set payout amount upon retirement like a pension plan does. Your payout will depend on how much you contributed over the years, if and how much your employer contributed, and how well the investments did. Unlike a pension plan, you have a great deal of control over your account and can decide how much of it to invest in mutual funds, annuities, money-market funds or your company's stock. If your employer offers a retirement plan, you really should take advantage of the opportunity.

Why? It's free money! Impossible, you say? No. Here's how you get free (and legal) money for very little effort:

- **Tax free.** Contributions to defined-benefit plans are tax-free. Your monthly contribution goes into your retirement account before withholding taxes are applied. This lowers your tax bill. And because you are not taxed on the earnings until you take them out, you have lots of years of compounding interest in your favor.

- **Automatically deducted.** Your contributions can be automatically deducted every month, so you don't "feel" the loss.

- Some employers even contribute to the plan. If yours does, make sure you contribute enough to get the highest allowable contribution from your employer. This truly is FREE MONEY and you need to make the most of it.
- Most of these plans involve no fees.

To Participate or Not to Participate?

Rachel is 23 and newly employed. She knows that participating in her employer's retirement program is important, but she is trying to save money for her upcoming wedding. What should she do? Let's just look at her first year of employment.

OPTION A:	OPTION B:
Contribute $1,200 (or $100/month) Leave the contribution in the retirement account until age 60. **Total: $21,550**	Don't contribute the $1,200. Pay taxes (18% federal, 4% state, in this case). **Total: $940**

These two options are conservative. Option A could potentially net much more money—if Rachel's employer matched her contributions, she would have more than double the $21,550 by the time she was 60. Also, the account may well earn above 8% interest. Option B, on the other hand, would be even further reduced with other standard deductions.

Other things you should know about employer-sponsored plans:

Employer match option. Some employers match a certain, stated percentage of your contribution—typically between 50 and 100 percent—up to 6 percent of your annual gross salary. If your employer matches, take it to the limit! Contribute as much as it takes to get their maximum contribution. Yes, this is redundant with the bullet point above, but it's that important. Not convinced? Think about it this way: The average raise is 4%. If your employer matches up to 6%, you are basically getting a 6% raise, tax-free!

Contribution limits. In 2007, you can contribute as much as $15,500 pre-taxes to your retirement account. That amount is set to adjust $500 for inflation every year, so that in 2008 you'll be able to contribute $16,000, and so on.

Vesting. Vesting refers to your ownership rights to your retirement money. You are fully vested in your own contributions. Any money you invest into a 401(k) at Company B will be yours when you move on to Company L. However, if your employer provides matching funds, those do not vest until you've proven you're going to stick around for a while. Each company has its own vesting schedule, but it's likely that, after one year you'd be partially vested (maybe 10% or so), after two years a little more vested (perhaps 20%), and so on. For many companies, you need to hang in for at least five years before you can take all the matching funds with you when you go. Be aware of your employer's vesting schedule; if you want to leave the company but it's just a matter of months before you're more fully vested, it might be worth sticking around so that when you do leave you can take more of that free money with you.

Changing jobs. When you change jobs you keep everything you've contributed to your retirement account. As we mentioned above, you may or may not get to keep the funds your employer has contributed, but what you have deposited is all yours. So, what do you do with your 401(k) when you switch to a new employer? Read on to learn the basics of rollovers.

Rollovers. This gets really complicated, so we'll just provide an overview here and some good sources where you can learn more about this topic. When you have a 401(k) set up with an employer and then you switch jobs, you have a few options for handling that retirement money:

- You can leave it alone if you're happy with how it's performing at Former Employer, or
- You can transfer it—roll it over—to your 401(k) at New Employer, or
- You can roll it over to an IRA, or
- You can take the money and run.

That last one sounds tempting, but it's a bad, bad idea. When you withdraw your retirement money early you get taxed, then penalized. Whoosh! You withdraw $1,000 and walk away with about $750 (depending on your tax bracket). That's not even counting all those lost future potential earnings our friend Lao Tzu revealed to us earlier.

Now, assuming you choose any of the three other ideas—all of them good, compared to #4—you need to deal with *how* to roll over that money. If you can avoid touching it, you're going to be in good shape. In other words, if Former Employer cuts you a check, then you transfer that check to your new 401(k) or IRA, you'll encounter withholding taxes. You'll get the money back at tax time, but you may have to fork out of your own pocket to transfer the whole amount or face penalties. And, if you don't perform the rollover within 60 days, you'll have to pay the 10% early withdrawal penalty. In order to avoid any penalties and taxes, you need to avoid touching the money at all by completing what's called a trustee-to-trustee transfer. Your human resource department at your current or new employer can help walk you through this process.

Withdrawing early. When you withdraw from your 401(k) you get hit with income tax *and* a 10% penalty. Ouch. There goes all that compounded interest. Do anything you can to avoid touching your retirement until you reach the age 59 ½ (the magic age the Government determined you can begin accessing your retirement funds).

Borrowing from your retirement. Many plans allow you to borrow from yourself, but it can be hazardous to your long-term financial health. These loans usually involve fees, operate on a strict and short repayment plan (generally within five years, though if you're borrowing for a down payment on a house you might have more time to pay yourself back), and require you to pay interest as determined by your plan administrator.

Self-employed and small business plans

If you are self-employed or work for a small business, there are several retirement plan options available to you.

Simplified Employee Pension (SEP): A SEP is great for someone who is self-employed and has no employees. Yes, only the employer can contribute to the plan, but you are your own employer, right? Therefore, you can contribute up to 15% of your earnings, up to a maximum of $40,000 a year. This is deducted off the top of your income (read: tax break!). Some states even allow the deduction from state taxes, too. Warning: Watch your contribution date. The IRS cares.

If you are an employee of a small business that participates in a SEP program, just know that there is one drawback: Your employer has complete control of your contribution level.

Savings Incentive Match Plan (SIMPLE): Businesses with fewer than 100 employees sometimes offer a SIMPLE plan. The key letter in this acronym is "M." Match. Employees with this plan can contribute up to $10,000—tax deferred—annually, and the employer must match 100%, up to 3% of annual gross compensation. Even if you don't make your own contribution (Huh? Give up free money?), the employer must contribute 2% of your salary, up to a maximum of $3,200.

Keogh Plans

Also referred to as money-purchase or profit-sharing plans, Keoghs are tax-deferred pension plans for those with self-employment income. They are complicated, paper-intensive, and best used under the supervision of a financial professional.

Individual Retirement Accounts (IRAs)

If your employer doesn't offer a retirement program—or if you're hooked on saving for retirement and want to sock away even more money—an IRA may be perfect for you. IRAs are, as the name implies, *individually* directed. Whereas an employer's 401(k) plan gives you a range of options within a program, an IRA is your creation. There are two types of IRAs, traditional and Roth.

Traditional IRA: Like the 401(k), a traditional IRA is tax-deferred—you don't pay taxes until you withdraw the money and in many cases you can deduct what you do contribute. In order to set up an IRA formally, work with a bank, financial planner, or mutual fund company. It's not terribly complicated, but will require precise documentation in order to maintain the tax-deferred status. Things to know about the Traditional IRA:

- **Expect fees.** As with any financial decision, shop around, get advice, and go with a well-respected organization you can trust.

- **Early withdrawal.** Know that early withdrawal means a hefty tax bill as well as substantial penalties.

- **Single person options.** If you are single and not participating in an employer-sponsored plan, you can put up to $4,000 a year into your IRA and deduct the full amount on your tax return. If you are single and you do participate in an employer-sponsored plan, you can put up to $4,000 a year into your IRA and deduct the full amount if your adjusted gross income is $50,000 or less (in 2007). If your income is higher, your deduction is prorated accordingly.

- **Married person options.** If you are married, filing jointly, your deduction eligibility depends on your income and whether you and/or your spouse already take part in an employer-sponsored plan. Check with the IRS website or a tax professional to figure out the limits and deductions that apply to your specific situation.

Note that contribution levels and eligibility requirements change from year to year. For the most current information, check with the IRS at www.irs.gov.

Roth IRA: You set up a Roth IRA with a bank, financial planner, or mutual fund company, just as you would a traditional IRA. But the Roth is quite different from the traditional IRA. First, you pay into a Roth with plain old after-tax dollars. No pre-tax contributions, no tax deductions. So, why go Roth? Well, it might pinch a little at first, but it feels really good later when you withdraw your money—and pay no taxes.

It's an oversimplification to suggest that choosing between a traditional IRA and a Roth IRA is simply choosing between paying taxes now or later. Because you're not paying the same taxes. With a traditional IRA, you don't know what rate you'll be paying because you don't have a crystal ball to tell you what tax bracket you'll be in and what the tax code of year 2071 will look like. And, of course, you'll be taxed on the account earnings. With a Roth, you pay up front according to your current tax rate, then your money grows tax-free.

Things to know about the Roth IRA:

- **Expect fees.** Shop around. Inform yourself.
- **Early withdrawal.** You can withdraw your money early without penalties if you're 59½ and have held the account for at least 5 years.
- **Benefacting.** You are not required to take your money out of a Roth when you reach age 70½ , so you can leave the money, if you are inclined, tax-free to your heirs. Traditional IRAs do not allow this.
- **Eligibility rules.** If you're single and your adjusted gross income exceeds $114,000 (2007 figure) or if you're married, filing jointly, and your income exceeds $166,000, good for you but you don't meet the eligibility rules for a Roth IRA.

As with the traditional IRA, you can find the best information about Roth IRA eligibility by going straight to the source—the IRS website (www.irs.gov).

This is a lot of information to take in and it can be overwhelming. Even though we've included a lot of details here, the best thing you can do now is to stop reading, ruminating, planning, and weighing options. Just act. Start participating now. Maybe you don't have your dream job or your "real" job yet—no matter. Don't wait until everything lines up perfectly. Take what you can afford now, and put it into an interest-bearing account. If you work for an employer that does automatic contributions, definitely sign up, even if it's for a modest amount. At some point, you've got to take the single step to start the journey. If you take it now, you'll thank yourself later.

Chapter 7

The Get Outta' Debt Plan

Since we're dealing with the heart-stopping, palm-sweating topic of debt, let's start with a non-threatening exercise of association. Ready? OK, if your debt were an animal, what kind of animal would it be? And if your debt were a sound, what sound would it be? Last one: If your debt were a building, what kind of building would it be?

If you responded "gnat," "silence," and "model gazebo," you do not need this chapter. Move on to the Saving for Retirement chapter or, better yet, the What It's Like to Be Completely Different from Other Members of My Generation chapter. Seriously, congratulations.

Now, if you answered that your debt "animal" would be a wolf, your debt "sound" would be a howl, and your debt "building" would be a jail, this chapter is for you.

Here's what you won't get if you read on: A quick fix or a magic bullet. But you also won't get a guilt trip. We assume you already know the basics about debt and are at the point where you need some simple reinforcements to keep you focused on a debt-free or at least low-debt future. We also assume you're ready to face the debt you accrued during college and are looking forward to digging yourself out of the hole, whether that hole is a product of uncontrollable circumstances, spending habits, or a combination of both.

What you need now is a refresher on the types of debt you probably face, how to tackle that debt, and resources to help you along the way. So for now just ignore the strange animal sounds and concentrate not on what has been but what is and will be.

The good, the bad, and the ugly

We promised no guilt trips and we'll keep that promise, but we need to use some judgment words in order to outline the types of debt you likely face. Financial advisors and other money experts, including the loan officer who may someday decide if you're a good candidate for a low-interest home loan, generally see debt that works as an investment and has tax advantages as good. Student and home loans tend to be "good" debt.

It's important to remember that your student loan *is* an investment. Even if you owe $25,000 for a degree in one of those fields not generally known as lucrative, say philosophy, you will experience a pay off. It may be nonmaterial, but likely it will entail some material gain as well. Statistically, people with post-secondary degrees do much better in the job market than those who don't have them.

Because of the importance of a college education, student loans are generally viewed as low interest, high return investments. Much like home loans, they promise higher future income. Also, both of these types of debts offer tax advantages—you can write off a portion of the interest, which pulls down the cost of the debt itself.

That's the good. Now for the bad and the ugly. First, credit cards. Credit card debt is not necessarily bad or ugly in and of itself. In fact, some credit card use is necessary and good for building your FICO score. Also, using credit cards for some purchases gives you extra insurance. And credit cards tend to be much better than cash when you travel and want to get the best exchange rate.

Credit card debt is bad debt, however, when it involves a double-digit interest rate and you're only able to make the minimum payment every month. Credit card debt is also bad when it's the product of living beyond one's means. Again, no guilt trip—the boots have been purchased and the weekend trip to Paduka is a distant memory—but if you're reading this chapter you're ready to avoid further frivolous charges on your credit card. So when to use the card? The car breaks down and you have no other way to pay for it? OK, put it on the card. Last year's snowboard isn't as cool as this year's model? Keep the plastic tucked away.

When is credit card debt downright ugly? The ugliness depends on how much you owe. How long will it take you to pay the debt down? How high is the interest rate? Is it limiting other opportunities, like your ability to apply for a home loan? The answers to those questions will tell you when your credit card load has moved from bad to ugly. Other debt that's just plain ugly is money owed to pay day loan companies and the mafia. We'll cover the former in a bit. (For the latter you're on your own.)

Get a handle on your debt

Like many money-related issues, it is easier to talk or read about debt, than to actually face it. But you've made a commitment to keep reading and we assume you're ready to look at the big picture. So here's how to tackle debt:

Step 1: Figure out what you owe. Pull out your latest credit card and student loan statements and compile a list of the following: amount you owe to each vendor, the interest rates, and your minimum monthly payments.

Beware the Minimum Monthly Payment

Consider This...

Consider Jill: She owes $1,000 at 18% interest to Credit Card Z. If she pays the monthly minimum, it will take 153 months to pay that baby off—and she'll pay a total of $1,115 in interest. That's right, more than double her initial debt load.

If Jill pays a fixed amount of just $40 a month, which is more than twice the initial minimum monthly payment required, it will take 32 months to pay off the card and she'll pay $262 in interest. Still not ideal, but much better than the first scenario.

(Note: Go to **www.nslds.ed.gov**, the National Student Loan Data System website, to see all of your student loans in one handy place.)

Step 2: Prioritize pay offs. You need to make the minimum monthly payments on all debts or your credit score will get dinged up. But, creditors' required minimum monthly payments are designed to pad their pockets and raid yours, so figure out how to pay more than the minimum. Pay off higher interest loans first. If Card A has an 18% rate, Card B has a 12% rate, and your student loans are at 7%, pay the minimum on the student loans and Card B, but pay Card A off as quickly as possible. If you type "debt calculator" into a search engine, you'll find some free calculating tools that will be helpful for this step.

Step 3: Consolidate debt. We don't necessarily mean to consolidate your debt "officially," using a for-profit company to manage your accounts. After all, those places have to make their profit from somebody, and you would end up paying out more money—sometimes significantly more—than if you took care of it on your own. If you can pull all of your credit card debt onto one low-interest card, do it. It will lower your overall interest payments and allow you to pay one bill instead of several, thereby increasing the odds of paying the bill on time and keeping your credit score up.

Step 4: Stay focused. Make it your mission to pay down debt and keep your charts, goals, and other notes in plain sight so you don't forget the big picture. Not only will you be in a better financial place later if you tackle debts now, you'll also experience mental and emotional relief when you take control of the issue.

Consider This ...

Should I raid my savings to pay off debt?

The answer to this question varies depending on the situation. Savings accounts tend to earn about 3%, while credit cards often charge 12% or even more. Simple math says that you'll end up keeping more of your money if you pay off the high interest debt faster. Ask: Have I kicked the habits that racked up the credit card debt? If the answer is no, then you need to be cautious about draining your savings because you could find yourself in more debt and without a safety net down the line, especially if you're faced with an unforeseen emergency expense that requires you to rack up credit expenses you just paid off. And when it comes to paying off student loans with savings, most financial advisors say to hold off, though your individual situation might give you reason to consider that option. As for the retirement account...do everything you can to maintain it! (See the Saving for Retirement chapter for all the reasons not to withdraw retirement early.)

How to deal with your student loan when you're no longer a student

If you're like many well-educated people in your generation, you not only have a degree, you also have approximately $19,237.38 in student loan debt. More if you attended a private college. Because of the ever-increasing costs of tuition and housing (and $200 textbooks!), a majority of graduates leave school with a diploma and a hefty load of student loans. For many, the debt they carry is absolutely staggering.

So what do you do with those loans now that you're out of school and actually expected to pay them back? One idea is to wrap a large monument—say, the Statue of Liberty—with loan statements and lecture notes, then make a documentary about the experience. You'll become a famous artist and your worries will be reduced to figuring out "the nature of postmodern experience." But that idea's already taken, so the best approach to your student loans is to pay them back.

Luckily, student loans are a pretty forgiving species: If you experience financial hardship you can make a quick phone call, fill out a form, and—voila!—you'll qualify for a deferment or forbearance. On the other hand, if you default on a student loan you'll look really, really flaky, experience a drop in your credit score, and might even have your wages garnished, a friendly word that means "your paycheck is our paycheck."

> **TIP**
>
> **Should I pay off student loans early?**
>
> Yes! If you can, and other "bad" debt is paid off, and you've invested in retirement, by all means pay down that student loan. Important tip: Make sure you note on the payment that your intention is to pay down the principal, not just make an early payment.

If you feel swamped with student loan debt and are unable to keep up with the payments, no matter how much you cut living expenses, you have options for getting out of the mire:

Deferment. A deferment is a temporary "get out of monthly payments" pass. People interested in pursuing this option need to apply and qualify for it. If you have a subsidized student loan and qualify for a deferment, interest will not accrue while you're deferring the loan. If you have an unsubsidized loan, interest will accrue, but your responsibility for payments will be postponed until later. To qualify for a deferment, you need to prove you are one of the following:

- still in school, or
- unemployed, or
- suffering from economic hardship, or
- active duty military.

Note: Peace Corps and AmeriCorps volunteers may be eligible to defer their loans while in service and almost certainly qualify for forbearance (see below).

Forbearance. Let's say you're not eligible for a deferment but still feel strapped by your student loan responsibilities. If this is the case, consider requesting a forbearance, which will allow you to postpone or reduce your monthly payments for a period of time (up to 12 months), while you get your footing. There are fewer obstacles to obtaining forbearance than a deferment. You need to demonstrate you are one of the following:

- in poor health, or
- in a rigorous residency, or
- paying 20% or more of your monthly income to student loan debt.

Lenders see forbearance as a win-win situation. When they allow you to put your loan in forbearance, they collect more money from you. Unlike deferred subsidized loans, interest accrues during the period of forbearance. Also, it's common to stretch out the length of the loan to reduce monthly minimums, which benefits the borrower in the short term and gives the lender more money over the life of the loan.

Consolidating student loans

When your student loan debt seems overwhelming, either because of the amounts involved or the number of bills you have to track each month, you might want to consider consolidating it. This is a popular method for dealing with student loans, though it isn't right for everybody.

Should You Consolidate?

Plug in your own numbers using an online calculator: **www.federalconsolidation.org http://loanconsolidation.ed.gov/loancalc**

Loan consolidation is the process of combining all current eligible loans into one. You end up with a fixed average interest rate and one monthly payment, which is generally lower than your current combined payments. To calculate interest, the lender uses a weighted average of your current loans and rounds it up ⅛%. The interest rate for consolidated loans is currently capped at 8.25%. You also have a menu of repayment options:

- **Standard plan:** Fixed payment. Repay within 10 years.
- **Extended plan:** Fixed payment. 12 – 30 years to repay.
- **Graduated repayment plan:** Payments begin small and increase with time (as you hope your income will increase). Up to 30 years to repay.
- **Income contingent plan:** Payment amount varies, depending on your income and loan balance. Up to 25 years to repay.

The Perks of a Perkins

GOOD TO KNOW

If you have a Perkins or other special, more-difficult-to-qualify-for loan, remember you'll lose benefits if you consolidate it. That nice, long grace period? Gone when consolidated. The lower interest rate? Averaged. And adios to any cancellation benefits. (Example: Some states offer loan forgiveness if you teach in a high-need area for a year or two. But consolidated loans are not eligible for these deals.)

But there is a catch: The weighted average might not change your payments drastically. Also, the life of the loan will be increased in order to get to a low monthly payment. In short, you pay less monthly, but more in the long term. Also, you want to be careful which loans you consolidate, because some—like the Perkins, for example—have great benefits that you'll lose if you lump them with the riff raff.

Let's take a look at how this would work with hypothetical graduate Bill. Bill's current student loan debt looks like this:

Loan Amount	Type of Loan	Interest Rate	Number of Payments	Monthly Payment	Total Cost of Loan
$10,000	Unsubsidized Stafford	5.25%	120	$107	$12,875
$10,000	Unsubsidized Stafford	6.8%	120	$115	$13,809
$15,000	Subsidized Stafford	4.0%	120	$151	$18,224

His total monthly payment is $373 and the total he'll pay over the life of his loans, assuming he doesn't prepay them, is $44,908.

If Bill decides to consolidate, he would have a combined loan amount of $35,000. The weighted average calculates out to 5% and the amount he pays monthly as well as over the life of the loan depends on which repayment plan he chooses:

Loan Amount	Repayment Plan	Type of Loan	Number of Payments	Monthly Payment	Total Cost of Loan
$35,000	Standard	5.0%	120	$371	$44,547
$35,000	Extended	5.0%	240	$230	$55,436
$35,000	Graduated	5.0%	240	$185	$58,046

So if Bill goes for the lowest possible monthly payment now by consolidating and selects the graduated repayment plan, it will cost him an additional $13,000.

There are a lot of factors missing from this scenario. For instance, Bill might have reason to believe that his income is going to

Key Student Loan Resources

See what you owe and to whom at the National Student Clearinghouse website: **www.nslc.org**. Learn all about loan consolidation at the U.S. Department of Education's website: **www.loanconsolidation.ed.gov** (or call 1-800-557-7392).

To Do!

increase exponentially in a year or two, which will allow him to pay off all of his debt. Without a crystal ball you won't know your best option until decades have passed, but you have all the resources you need to make the decision that you think is best for you now.

Things to Keep in Mind if You Decide to Consolidate:

- You can only consolidate your student loans once (unless you go back to school and take on additional student loan debt).

- You don't have to consolidate all of your student loans into one.

- Receive a lower interest rate by
  - Consolidating during your student loan grace period (generally the first six months after you graduate or go less than full time).
  - Signing up for automatic debit payments.
  - Making on time payments for 36 months straight.

- Legit lenders do not charge fees for consolidation. If you are asked to pay a fee, you are working with the wrong company.

So this chapter could be summarized as follows: Debt might look like a dragon and sound like a hyena, but it's really just a pile of numbers you need to face and, sometimes, rearrange. Avoid adding to your debt and definitely pay over the minimum required and you will pull yourself out of the crevasse. Student loans offer more flexibility and grace than other debts; explore all options and remember that the only ugly one is defaulting.

Chapter 8

Set Goals & Make Trade-Offs

What do you want to be when you grow up? For a five-year-old, the response is usually effortless: A firefighter. A superhero. A ballerina and an elephant. As we get older, we change our answers, but still fixate on that one question, as if it's the only one that matters.

While other people may persist in asking what you are or what you want to be, it's time to change the questions you ask yourself. Your profession is important—especially if you did end up becoming a superhero—but *what* you are is less important than *who* you are. Questions that matter most to your life now are, *Who do I want to be?* and *What do I want to do?* In your search for the answers to these questions, you will need to reflect on your personal values. Part of this search entails understanding your relationship with money and figuring out how your life goals mesh with your financial goals.

It's time to spend a little time with your most trusted life coach and financial advisor: a pad of paper. If you have that, a pencil, and a little bit of time, you can begin to design the life you want.

Defining your goals

Setting clear goals gives you **vision** and **motivation**. TIP

Here's a start: Sit down and write a list of all the dreams and goals you have in mind. Be as specific as possible. Don't just write "travel" if what you really want is to "kayak the Amazon." Try to segment your goals into stages: think short term (today, this week, within the year), mid-range (1 – 5 years), and long-range (5 + years). Don't edit as you go—this list is for your eyes only and is subject to change.

All goals should
- be measurable
- have a timetable
- involve a strategy

TIP

Once you've compiled a comprehensive list, go through it and check all of the items related to money. Then begin a second list, with your money-related goals arranged in order of importance. As you prioritize, edit and refine.

You're much more likely to achieve a goal if it's specific, measurable and involves an action plan and timetable. It's not enough to say "I want to be independently wealthy." What does "wealthy" mean? (Having a thousand dollars in the bank? Owning a medium-sized city? Controlling Dubai from a manmade, charmingly dolphin-shaped island?) When do you want to achieve this? (In 40 years? By next Thursday?) How will you accomplish it? (Redesigning the talking beer bottle opener? Selling bonds? Teaching English as a second language in Madison, Wisconsin?)

Benefits of Goal-Setting

Consider This ...

Coaches, corporate advisors, and academics agree that people who set clear, measurable goals for themselves tend to be more focused, more self-confident, and more successful.

Make sure you include the occasional splurge in your short-term goals—you should enjoy your first paid vacation, for instance, and you may want a few new outfits to celebrate your first real job. If you treat yourself occasionally in this way, you will be more likely to save and reach those long-term goals.

Keep your goal worksheet in a handy place so you can check and revise it periodically.

Example Financial Goals Worksheet

Goal	Money Needed	Strategy	Timeline
1. Pay off student loans	$16,000	• Consolidate loans • Make extra payment of $125/month	December 2010
2. Buy a "starter" home in the North End	$30,000 for down payment	• Build excellent credit score • Telecommute two days a week; put transportation savings toward house • Save $400 per month in dedicated account • Once student loan is paid off, contribute same amount toward down payment account	June 2012

Making trade-offs

Now that you've pinned your dreams to paper, you might feel overwhelmed. There are so many things to do, places to go, purchases you want to make, yet you're already incredibly busy and perhaps pressured by debt. Your salary's anemic, your "need" list long, your "want" list longer, the car's due for a tune-up, and it looks like you won't be able to afford a real vacation until 2020, when you finally drag that kayak to the Amazon.

Take a breath.

You can't do it all right now. Just do one thing. And no crash money diets—they work about as well as crash food diets (which is to say, they don't work at all). As with many things in life, you need to find a financial balance that will allow you to enjoy life in the present as you prepare for the future.

Make trade-offs along the way. You might decide, for example, to keep driving the junker for two years longer than originally planned, in order to save more money for a down payment on a house. Or you might find that your original entertainment budget of $8 a month was too stringent, as it barely covered the price of your favorite lychee martini.

Your goals for the future are meant to motivate and inspire you, not change you into a hermit. Build in some expenses for pleasure. If you switch from eating out every day to packing lunches, for example, you can go out for happy hour on Friday and still come out $25 ahead. Sure, if you cut back on all social dining you'd reach one of your long-term big goals a little sooner; you decide what the trade-off is worth.

To Do: Take Action

To Do!

Feeling antsy? Want to stop sitting around writing out goals, dreaming up plans, and designing spreadsheets? Good. Here are some things you can do right now to fire up your action plan:

- Check on your retirement account. Figure out what percentage it's earned the past quarter and year.
- Call your bank to ask if there are checking account options you're not using that will help you save some money. (For example, will you get free checking if your paycheck is deposited automatically?)
- Set up online payments for every merchant who accepts them.
- Cancel your landline if you really just use your cell phone.
- Turn off lights you aren't using.
- Place unwanted items up for sale on Craigslist or eBay.

Revisit your long-term goals frequently to remind yourself that the way you earn, spend, and keep your money is a personal choice. Some of your goals will require more effort and you can expect unforeseen obstacles, but remember: You can do it. You survived puberty, right? What's better proof of resilience than that?

Chapter 9

Making Personal Finances Personal

Time for some meta-visualization. (Sometimes we have to throw in those terms so our parents know all those years at college taught us something). Imagine yourself in the future—take it three years out, then ten years, then thirty. Are you active? Productive? Fulfilled? Energized? Engaged in meaningful work? (Yes, it sounds like an infomercial, but you are visualizing, after all, so might as well do it up. Give yourself white teeth, good knees, and a full head of hair while you're at it.) And what does your financial picture look like out there in the future? Are you solvent? Can you afford to travel/pay for the kids' braces/contribute to your favorite causes?

Good. Now let's talk about making that happen. The most significant first step is to realize that you are in control. You. Not your parents or your boss or the student loan company with the cheerfully hip graphics on its website. Sure, you are tied to others in this world and indebted to some, but you have power no matter how broke you are or how much debt you have. You control your knowledge, actions, and attitude.

Know what to know

Knowledge is power: It's cliché because it's true. What's in your account is less important than what's in your brain. A lot of people, however, don't really like to think about money beyond "If I had more, I could…." If you want to get to that place you visualized earlier, you've got to think about finances frequently and deliberately. This is not about being greedy or money-hungry, but about taking care of the inevitable business side of life so that it doesn't "take care" of you.

Here's how to get control of your finances through knowledge:

1. Understand your relationship with money (see below).
2. Know what's coming in and what's going out.
3. Understand how your remaining income is working for you.
4. Inform yourself using reputable sources: Ask questions; read articles, books, and websites; go to the occasional seminar or workshop.
5. Do Steps 1 – 4 in no particular order, over and over and over again.

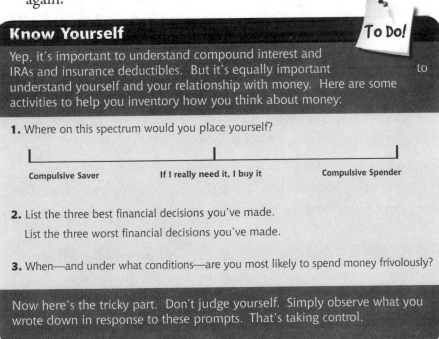

Know Yourself   **To Do!**

Yep, it's important to understand compound interest and IRAs and insurance deductibles. But it's equally important to understand yourself and your relationship with money. Here are some activities to help you inventory how you think about money:

1. Where on this spectrum would you place yourself?

|⌐_____|_____⌐|

Compulsive Saver   If I really need it, I buy it   Compulsive Spender

2. List the three best financial decisions you've made.
List the three worst financial decisions you've made.

3. When—and under what conditions—are you most likely to spend money frivolously?

Now here's the tricky part. Don't judge yourself. Simply observe what you wrote down in response to these prompts. That's taking control.

It sounds like a full-time job, but it doesn't have to be. Don't worry about reading every prospectus and article you come across. Just do what you can when you can and you'll learn as you go. It's worth making your financial self-education a priority. You work hard; it'd feel great to make the most of your earnings.

Know the best sources

Finding information is not a problem. Plug the phrase "best mutual funds" into your search engine and you'll get about 16,000,000 hits. Even if researching mutual funds is your full time job, you need to know how to identify the truly useful information or you'll drown in the mire of the Web, where little Kaylee Drebber's 5th grade research project and Ted Hairproduct's financial evangelism pop up right next to Forbes and the Better Business Bureau.

Separate the useful from the useless (and determine affiliation and bias) by following these tips:

- **Ask people you know and trust.** What sources do they rely on for financial information?

- **Read articles that apply to you.** If you have time to learn about onion futures, go for it. But if you're schedule is tight, focus on the material that will benefit you immediately.

- **Check authorship.** Who wrote the piece? Who published it? Many for-profit websites contain helpful information, but if you're learning about the art of CD laddering from a bank website, expect an underlying sales pitch.

- **Notice advertising.** If the cute, toothy financial guru gets advertising dollars from James K. Polk Investments, his advice might tilt toward the advertiser even if it's not the best choice for his audience.

- **Find "go-to" sources.** Pick three or four resources, such as books or websites, that have proven to be helpful, thorough, and accurate. That way, when you're doing some rushed researching, you'll get solid answers fast.

- **Check three.** Before you make any financial decision, check with at least three trusted sources. Even if you have a financial advisor, you need to ensure you're well informed and have the tools to make sound decisions.
- **Go slow.** If it's a hot deal and you've got to act fast or you'll lose out...pass. Any decision you make will involve a degree of uncertainty, but pinning all hopes on the sounds-too-good-to-be-true opportunity is like believing that, if you're really, really nice this year, Santa will swoop down and pay off your student loans.

Financial personal trainers and certified financial advisors

There are benefits to working with a financial advisor: They save you time, might get higher returns than you would on your own, and provide an objective view that can help keep you focused on your financial goals.

It might feel strange to entrust your finances to a third party. It *should* feel strange—there's significant risk involved. Arm yourself with some basic knowledge and you'll be fine.

The good financial coach...

- Has strong references.
- Helps, advises, sympathizes, and praises.
- Asks first: What are your goals? What financial problems do you have? What assets and liabilities do you have?
- Develops a workable strategy and reviews it regularly with you.
- Contacts you regularly.

Beware of the financial advisor who...

- Asks first: How much money do you have to invest?
- Asks you to make out checks to him or her personally. Except for fees, all checks for investments should be in the name of the brokerage or mutual fund.
- Lists him or herself as a joint owner or beneficiary on any of your accounts.

- Signs your name to documents.
- Does not contact you regularly.

How do Financial Planners Earn a Living?

Here are the most common ways financial planners make money:

1. **Commissions.** Commission-based planners get money from brokerages every time they sell a product to you. Analogy: If you go to a Honda dealership, they're going to try to sell you a Honda, even if the best car for you is actually a Volkswagon.

2. **Fees.** Fee-based planners charge a percentage of the assets they are helping you manage. The bigger the assets, the more they make. Some of these planners won't take on clients who don't meet a minimum asset threshold.

3. **Combination of Fees and Commissions.** Some planners charge to develop a plan, then collect commissions by selling you the things the plan comprises. Analogy: You buy a car from a dealer—we'll call him a Transportation Consultant—who receives a fee for selling to you, then collects commission on every gallon of gas you put into that car.

4. **Hourly/Flat Rates.** These planners charge you for their time, either by the hour or with a flat rate. They meet with you and help you develop a plan. You can follow through on the plan on your own or pay them more to do the legwork for you. These tend to be the least biased, but it does require more time on your part as well as more up-front money.

As an alternative, you don't have to hire a paid consultant or certified financial advisor. Solid help can come from a friend, relative, coworker—someone you trust and who has experience and sound financial judgment. There is a lot of free wisdom to be had just by asking. Do protect yourself—and your relationship with this trusted person—by always following up any advice with your own research. That way you'll gain confidence in your own judgment. Plus, you'll be able to give yourself some credit for the good decisions and won't be tempted to blame your "trainer" if an investment bonks.

If you do decide to work with a paid professional, start your research by asking friends and family for their recommendations.

Interviewing a Prospective Planner

When you interview a financial advisor, take your time and
don't be shy about asking questions. It's a big commitment and
you will feel more confident if you're thorough at this stage of the process.
Following are important questions to ask:

- How do you charge for your services?
- Do you perform other services, like tax or legal advising?
- What qualifies you to be my financial coach?
- How long have you been a financial planner?
- How many clients do you have? How big is the asset base you manage for those clients?
- What kind of liability insurance do you carry?
- Do you currently work with clients in a comparable financial situation to mine?
- Can you give me references?
- Once the plan is complete, how will I implement it?

Action and attitude

All of the advice seeking and research should go a long way toward making you feel like an informed, capable investor and consumer. If you tend to act rashly, you might have to train yourself to take the time to investigate your options. If, on the other hand, you're the type who could research, take notes, cross-reference, and analyze for months before making a decision, remember the risks of inaction such as lapsed health insurance, or loss of earnings. Same advice goes for relationships, but that's for another book.

Getting to that glorious, financially solvent future requires research, action, and a confident attitude. Confidence here means you can look squarely at your current financial situation and make a plan for your future one. It's really not so much about taking control as it is about recognizing—and acting upon—the control you already have.

Chapter 10

Increase Your Salary

The nip-and-tuck approach to finances—cutting coupons and eating off-brand rice and beans—only takes you so far. At some point, you just want to make more money. There are plenty of ways to increase your income, though not all of them are pleasant or legal. Some people take second jobs, start a side business, sign up to be medical test subjects at the local university, or sell their roommate's stuff on eBay. A better, often overlooked way to make more money is simply to ask your boss for a raise.

We're not suggesting you march into your boss's office after a week on the job and declare it's high time for a pay increase. However, after you've been at your job for six months, it's good to reflect on where you are and what you're doing for the organization. If you deserve a raise, ask for it, and get it, that little conversation with your boss could translate into a salary increase of several thousand dollars or more. And it would probably be less painful than enduring another sleep deprivation study at the local U or your best friend's wrath when he discovers his shark tooth collection has been shipped off to Paduka.

Probably less painful. Depends on the boss, doesn't it? If you look through the Sunday comics you'll see all sorts of throwback images of what happens when a person requests a raise. Man nervously asks for raise, boss chomps on cigar, boss laughs, man pleads, boss kicks him in the tush, man goes home to a nice wife and a towering sandwich. That's not going to happen to you. (Except, maybe, the sandwich part.)

Sure, you could get turned down. So? "No" is the second-best answer you could get. Don't jump in quite yet, though. Requesting a raise is a process that involves a lot of thought and preparation before you even make the appointment to talk with your boss.

Do you deserve a raise?

This is the guiding question. We all want more money and can imagine everything we'd do with a plumped-up paycheck, but when you ask for increased compensation you need to prove you really deserve it—first to yourself, then to your boss.

You deserve a raise if you…

- consistently exceed expectations
- have increased skills and education since you started the job
- perform significant duties beyond those outlined in your job description
- frequently work overtime in order to complete projects

When you are certain that you've performed at a level worthy of increased compensation, you'll be in a better position to sell your boss on the idea. The next step is to determine a fair salary for your work.

How much are you worth?

You have unique, inherent qualities that make you a special being interconnected with the other beings of this planet. Unfortunately, you don't get a paycheck for any of that.

Your "worth," as we're using the word here, is the amount your organization's willing and able to spend to employ you. Determining factors include your skills, education, and performance on the job, as well as organization, industry, and regional standards.

Figuring out fair compensation for your work takes algebraic grace and some research. Dig around to find out what others in your field are making. Good resources for expected salary range:

- Online salary calculators
- Professional organizations
- Your university's alumni and career services offices
- Want ads and on-line postings
- Your organization's human resources department
- Coworkers (be careful with this one!)

Don't dig too much with your coworkers. Be sensitive to the atmosphere of the office and your particular relationships with colleagues. Some organizations are very open, but in most environments salaries are confidential and it's a real impropriety to talk about them. If you do have information about coworkers' salaries, do not bring that up in your negotiations. It sounds whiny. Plus, you'll prove your individual merit better if you don't make comparisons to others.

GOOD TO KNOW

How much should I ask for?

You'll get a barrage of wildly different responses to this question from negotiating experts. The national average for raises is just under 4%. Your human resources department might be willing to divulge the company average; this would give you a sense of precedent and expectations.

Some experts recommend you ask for double what you really want. Others suggest a more conservative approach (asking for 7% when you know you'd be happy with 5%, for example).

If your job duties are drastically different from when you were first hired or if you discover in your research that you're significantly undervalued, you might swing a hefty pay increase.

Timing

So you've been at the job for six months, consistently do superior work, and have taken on more responsibilities. Is it a good time to ask for a raise? The answer is "yes" if...

- The organization seems to be on an up-swing: good earnings (if it's a publicly traded company this will be easy to find out), lots of new hires, and no shortage of resources.

- You have recently impressed others with your creativity, sales, performance, etc.
- Headhunters or representatives from another organization have been wooing you.
- You are due for your annual performance review. Note: it's easier to negotiate an increase in the amount offered at a performance review than to request a meeting and review mid-cycle.
- The region's job market is strong.

The answer is "maybe not" if...

- The organization isn't doing well. Vacated desks, low earnings, rationed sticky notes, and scandalous news stories are all signs that it might not be the best time to ask for more money.
- You have recently screwed up.
- The region's job market is weak.

Once you've determined that the organization could probably afford to raise your pay (or that you're so good they can't afford not to), there's another bit of timing to consider: when to approach your boss. Schedule an appointment with him or her so that you'll have adequate time to present your case.

How to be persuasive

Most of us mastered the art of persuasion by practicing on our parents. Let's travel back in time. You're in high school and you want something from your parents. No, not unconditional love or wise counsel. You want to borrow the car because you have a date. And you believe you'll improve your chances of having a successful evening if you drive your parents' burgundy Honda rather than asking your date to hop on the back of your tricked-out, low-rider bicycle. What makes for a "successful" evening? Well, that depends on your perspective, which matters very much to you but is not necessarily something you want to share with your parents.

The Art of Persuasion
Know what you want and state it clearly

- Understand your audience: How will the boss and the organization benefit by giving you a raise?
- Support your argument with evidence. Provide documentation of accomplishments.
- Anticipate opposition and be prepared to counter it.
- Always maintain a calm, reasonable tone.

The best approach to getting what you want in this scenario is to focus on your audience's—in this case your parents'—wants or needs.

If you say, "Mom, I want the Honda tonight because it's gonna make me look hot and I need to look hot because I'm really hoping to impress this girl and maybe she'll want me to sing in her band and we'll road-trip around for a couple of years and then maybe have children...", well, let's just say that Mom is not going to agree to that.

Similarly, your boss doesn't want to know how a higher salary will help you afford a new car or pay off bills or take a trip to Europe. He or she wants to know how it will benefit the organization. Your task is to prove your value to him or her in a calm and reasonable manner, using documentation from your "Achievements and Accomplishments" file. Always, always remember that this is not personal; it's business. No tears, no temper.

And the answer is...

...usually not simple. You might get a resounding "Yes!" to your proposed increase, but it's more common to hear "Yes, if..." or "Maybe later..." or "Not right now..." or "How about this...." (Again, very similar to dealing with parents.)

The Line in the Sand

Be willing to back up everything you say. If you declare an ultimatum—If I don't get this raise, I'm walking—you have to be able to follow through on it. If you have other equally or more attractive options than your current job, then you're in a better bargaining position and can take more risks. However, if you're fairly happy at the company or don't have other viable options, keep the stakes lower.

This is why you prepared so much going into the meeting. You know what you want, why you're worth a higher salary, and what's at stake for you. What you are about to learn is what they can offer you. Maintain an open mind. Maybe the company can't afford the full amount you requested right now, but your boss is willing to let you telecommute twice a week or can offer you some other flexible work arrangement.

Sometimes bosses will counter a raise request with a slight pay increase and a new title; that might be a good option if you're thinking of moving on in the near future as it will show well on your resume.

Work with your boss to devise a plan to develop your expertise and improve your credentials so that you can move up in the organization or at least move up on the salary schedule. The best employer-employee relationships are mutually beneficial.

Salary negotiations can get complicated and confusing, so always be ready to say, "This is a lot to think about. I'd like some time to go over these ideas on my own. Can we meet tomorrow to talk about this some more?"

Negotiating is part art, part science, and part poker. Do everything in your power to demonstrate excellence on the job, document it, and then calculate what that's worth to you and your employer. Successful negotiations depend on being able to read the company climate as well as your particular audience, your boss. Then, of course, there's the leap: Declaring what you want and waiting for the reaction. Sure, there's a risk. But if you keep your cool during the process, there's little to lose and a lot to gain.

Chapter 11

Making a Great First Impression

Ten seconds. That's about how much time you have to make a lasting first impression. (It's actually a little less time than that, but we'll round it up to simplify things.) Whether you're on a date, at an interview, or on day one of a new job, those first ten seconds have to be good. No biggie, right? Just enroll in some acting classes, hire a vocal coach, work out like a fiend, and convince some cheery ex-model-type talk show host to treat you to a total wardrobe makeover. Oh, and buff the briefcase and shoes. Then sit back because you have it totally made. Right.

Here's the part where your blood pressure skyrockets while we tell you why humans are wired to make snap judgments and how it's really a good thing, a survival tactic we carry with us from the cave to the cubicle. Imagine, after all, the poor caveman who carefully deliberated, weighing the pros and cons of taking action when confronted by a charging bear. There are benefits to the quick appraisal: It saves time and energy. Also, our instincts are pretty reliable. We have inherent expertise that tells us, "Shifty eyes plus muttering plus clenched fists: bad. Nice eyes plus clear voice plus smile: very, very good." We don't have to take a body language seminar to know who's a potential threat and who's a potential mate.

Great, you say. Love the snap judgment when appraising, but it's a little nerve wracking to be the appraised. Plus, all this talk of bears and clenched fists raises the anxiety level a few notches. OK, relax. Because here's the part where we tell you what you can do to ensure you do make a great first impression on your new bosses and coworkers. And it doesn't involve a vocal coach or a total wardrobe makeover.

It does, however, mean debunking some favorite sayings, such as "Looks aren't everything" and "It's what's inside that counts." Yes, yes, but…the truth is that people judge on appearances first, then on personality and performance. So we have to pay attention to how we look and the impression we create.

Grooming and dress

Grooming and dress are the first things people notice about you, long before they know anything about your work ethic or crystalline brilliance. Luckily, it's fairly easy to manage this aspect of your image and it doesn't necessarily have to cost your first year's salary.

For any job, you'll want to present a well-groomed, well-shod self. There were exceptions to these basic rules in the mid-1990s, when

How to Wear It

Here are answers to your most common style questions:

Good To Know

- **How should my suit fit?** The jacket sleeves should hit your wrist bone when your arms are relaxed. About ½ inch of shirt should show beyond that.
- **What's the best blouse fit?** A good-fitting blouse will not pucker at the shoulders or chest. If it's a long-sleeved blouse it should hit your wrist bone.
- **What's the best trouser length?** Pants should rest on the top of your shoes in front and go about ½ inch down in the back. This rule applies equally to men and women, though some women's pants are cropped by design.
- **How many shirt buttons can I leave undone?** For men and women, leaving the top one or two buttons undone is generally acceptable.
- **What color socks should I wear?** Match pants, not shoes. Remember that socks should not be visible unless you're sitting down.
- **What's the best heel height?** Shoes with a 1 – 2 ½ inch heel are safe bet. In some organizations, higher heels will be acceptable.
- **Do I need to wear hose?** That depends on the organization. Bare legs and open-toed or peek-a-boo shoes are acceptable in many workplaces.
- **What's the best tie length?** The bottom of your tie should hit the spot between the top and bottom of your belt.
- **How should I accessorize?** Shoes and belt should match each other. Wear minimal jewelry.
- **What's the best skirt length?** Skirts should be knee length or longer.

employees took the looks-aren't-everything maxim to heart and were often spotted coming to work in what might best be termed "pajama casual." In most companies, however, the norm now is definitely a professional or laid-back professional (otherwise known as "business casual") look. So what should you wear? In some workplaces the dress code is obvious and might even be outlined in the employee handbook. In others the rules might be less clear and you'll see people in pinstripe suits working alongside those in jeans and sneakers. Dress according to what you see around you. Pay particular attention to the people who hold similar positions to yours: They are your most reliable resource when you're trying to figure out the wardrobe norms of the organization.

Even in a relatively casual office environment, it's worth dressing up a bit for the first few months of a new job. This is not to say that you need to wear a three-piece suit if everyone around you is in Bermudas and flip-flops. One lesson we all learned in the throes of fourth grade, after all, was that fitting in is important and

What's Your Company's Image?

Good To Know

Your interview and first visits to the company will probably give you a strong sense of the company's image and how you will fit in with it. The three most common modes of dress in today's workplace are Professional, Business Casual, and Creative. The definitions and descriptions of these categories do vary by company and region, but this chart is a good starting place for understanding your workplace's image.

Dress Mode	Definition	Environment
Professional	Suit or sport jacket with slacks/skirt Collared shirt Conservative accessories Tie (men) Hose (women)	Banking, law, medical, engineering, insurance, sales, management, and accounting
Business Casual	Slacks (cotton OK in some offices) Knee-length (or longer) skirt Collared shirt (including golf-style shirts) Tailored sweater Coordinated accessories Hose and close-toed shoes (required in some business casual environments)	Technology, education, journalism, retail, government, human services, and science
Creative	Anything goes (within the norms of the company culture)	Marketing, arts, and design

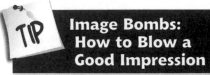

Image Bombs: How to Blow a Good Impression

Your company may have a liberal dress code—or no dress code at all—but there are some hard-and-fast rules to follow if you want to make a positive impression. Here's a quick list of the major DON'TS:

- **Don't show too much skin.** Both sexes: Make sure your V-neck is not too deep. Keep that chest—manly or womanly—under wraps. Also, all clothing should fit well and not be tight or clingy. Women: Avoid spaghetti straps and mini skirts.

- **Don't come on strong.** Both sexes: Douse yourself in perfume or cologne and you could turn people off and/or prompt an allergic reaction. Keep jewelry tasteful.

- **Don't let your clothes say too much.** Clothing with offensive, distasteful, or questionable slogans is best left in the back of the closet. One exception: If you're working for a political campaign, wearing a slogan-covered t-shirt might actually advance your career.

maybe even evolutionarily advantageous. However, in the case of your new job, it's better to err a little on the conservative side: A quick study of the best-dressed employee can reveal how to fit in while still projecting earnestness and ambition.

Now let's talk about the ever nebulous "casual day." What evil but brilliant clothing marketer came up with this concept? It's ambiguous at best, a cruel and misleading conspiracy at worst. Most of us, after all, have two types of casual: Painting the Town Red and Painting the House. Neither of these constitutes the "casual" in casual day, though if you look around the office you might see some silky chemises that would fit in well at a nightclub or, on the other hand, paint-bespattered, torn shorts that are one washing away from the rag pile.

Casual day is ripe for confusion. Usually, it means to dress comfortably without the sloppiness afforded by truly comfortable clothes. So you can wear jeans, but not the holey ones. "Dressy" T-shirts are OK, too. Again, the best guide to what's really appropriate is to consider how higher ups and well-dressed colleagues interpret the dress code. And when meeting with clients, definitely take your look up a few notches.

Maintaining a groomed workspace

Unlike the interview, your image now that you actually have the job is a product not just of how well you take care of yourself but also how well you take care of your space. The state of your desk, office, or cubicle (even your handbag and car, in some professions) factors into your overall impression on others.

There's no revelation here, just a reminder to keep things organized and clean, especially in those first few months when you're building others' opinions of and confidence in you. Even if you are chronically disorganized, pretend you are not. Spend time setting up your office or cubicle and clean out your wallet, purse, and briefcase. Coworkers can figure the truth out later, but by then they'll be charmed by you and think your clutter is a sign of character and creativity.

When it comes to decorating your workspace, keep this in mind: It's an extension of you, a "personalized public space," not a private space. Make it comfortable and personal. It's OK to show off your family and friends, but keep the party photos at home.

Non-verbal communication

Body language accounts for about half of what we say, and therefore comprises a huge part of our image. Try the following exercises to model this point. Stand with your arms crossed in front of you and eyes directed down at the floor. Say, "I'm so happy to meet you" in a cheerful voice. Or, cock your head to one side, raise an eyebrow, smile, and say, "I'll take a look at the data."

You're sending out signals all over the place. Your actual words, of course, count for some of what you say. But the tone of voice and body language you employ are much more significant indicators of your meaning. The most frequently cited study on interpersonal communication states that body language and facial expressions account for 55% of meaning, tone and quality of voice account for 38%, and the actual meaning of the words count for just 7%.

What's Your neutral position?

"In my early twenties, I realized there was a major discrepancy between how I saw myself and how others viewed me. People would come up to me at social events and say, 'Is everything OK?' and, 'You look bored' even when I thought I was having a great time. Then one evening I caught a reflection of myself having 'fun's: My mouth was a thin, straight line, my arms crossed over my chest, and my eyebrows were drawn together in a scowl. I looked like I was about to run an Antarctic marathon, not like someone having a good time at a party. After that, I learned to relax my face and stand casually, without crossed arms, and I think it's made me the approachable person I always thought I was." – **Kristy M., New York, NY**

Eye contact, posture, fidgeting…all of these non-verbal cues can really reinforce or sabotage what you verbalize. Be aware of what your body is saying at all times. You might even want to spend some time in front of a mirror, evaluating your "neutral position" (the way you carry yourself most of the time, when you're not actively engaged in conversation).

Here are some attributes of "positive" and "negative" body language:

"Positive" Body Language
(Signals interest, confidence, enthusiasm, and/or approachability)

- Nods head
- Uses hand gestures for emphasis (excessive gestures may signal aggression, however)
- Handshake is firm and confident
- Has erect posture
- Smiles
- Blinks at a regular rate
- Body takes up space (stance, posture, and arm position say, I belong here)
- Cocks head slightly (shows interest, but can be interpreted as confusion or flirtation)

"Negative" Body Language
(Signals boredom, insecurity, annoyance, and/or aloofness)

- Pins arms to side or across chest
- Handshake is limp or overpoweringly strong
- Slumps or hunches over
- Frowns, grimaces, or clenches jaw
- Expressionless, blank face
- Blinks too fast or stares
- Body closed off (stance, posture, and arm position say, I don't want to take up any space)
- Fidgets excessively
- Rolls eyes
- Yawns or sighs

While it's easy to adopt a professional wardrobe even if you've been living in workout wear for the last few years, it's challenging to makeover your body language. After all, you've had decades to adopt the unconscious quirks that make up your body language vocabulary. Also, your posture, expressions, and gestures are more indelibly you than a shirt or shoes, and can't—and shouldn't—be discarded willy-nilly.

A few adjustments, however, might help you in your professional life. If you tend to sit back with your arms crossed during meetings, you'll project disinterest and maybe even resistance to new ideas. Reminding yourself to sit upright and to lean forward a little when listening to others could project a radically different, and more successful, image. Just being more aware of your image will help you change it.

Verbal communication

Of course, while nonverbal communication accounts for an enormous part of one's image, verbal communication is still important. The average person says between 10,000 and 24,000 words a day. So what, exactly, are we saying?

The truth is that some people don't know what they're saying or how they're saying it. And communication skills are not optional, a bonus accessory some professionals happen to have; they are vital for every professional. Your success on the job is inextricably linked to the way you communicate.

What's your communication style? Do you say what you mean? Do you say it effectively? What do you inadvertently communicate to others when you talk to them? Take stock of your verbal communication skills and polish them if necessary—you'll be glad you did.

Communication styles can be influenced by a variety of factors, such as culture, gender, personality, and education. Everyone has his or her own personal style. Of course, that style is also dependent on audience: You probably won't use the same tone and vocabulary around your supervisor as you do your good friends. Understanding your own style as well as the different types you might encounter in others will give you an advantage in communicating with a broad range of people and will help you communicate more clearly. Here are some elements to consider:

- **Rate of speaking.** Do you speak rapid-fire or back-porch? If you speak too fast, you risk losing people and/or appearing insecure. If you speak too slowly, you risk boring people and/or appearing, well, slow. Confident people know that others will listen to them, so they don't rush through their sentences. Considerate people know that they are not the only ones with something important to say. Be both confident and considerate.

- **Volume and clarity.** You have good ideas and the skills to put them into action, but if you mumble you are creating an obstacle to your own success. Speak clearly, enunciate, and project confidence.

If you're really serious about auditing your verbal communication style, the best thing to do is to watch a videotape of yourself interacting with others. Keep an open and critical mind as you view the "evidence." Try to notice, not judge, your "ums," "ahs," "likes," and

The Power of Video Taping

"Two years ago, as part of a professional development program, I was assigned the task of videotaping myself at work. I'm an educational coordinator and speaking to small and medium-sized groups is what I do all day every day. You would think I'd be completely comfortable videotaping my work. Wrong. It made my stomach hurt just to think about it. And when I watched the DVD later, I really felt sick. 'I sound like Elmo! I look like a blob! Do I really say 'like' forty-four times a minute?' Once I got over the initial shock of seeing myself in action, I sat back and tried to evaluate my performance dispassionately. I say 'like' a lot. OK. Notice that. I tend to smile a lot when addressing a question. OK. Notice that. I started to see the video as information and then used that information to adjust some elements of my 'performance' at work. It was the most challenging but valuable professional development exercise I have ever done and I highly recommend it."

– Patrick C., Albuquerque, NM.

other inadvertent conversation habits. Consider these questions: How much time do you give to other speakers? Do you interrupt frequently, sometimes, or not at all? Is your voice audible? How do you physically present yourself? Many people find watching themselves on video about as pleasant as an appendicitis attack during rush hour traffic. If you can get past the initial horror you'll find it's an invaluable exercise.

Another helpful practice is asking a trusted friend or family member to give you some honest and constructive feedback. Or find a group like Toastmasters International (www.Toastmasters.org) that will provide an opportunity to practice public speaking in a non-threatening environment. It's a big—and for some, scary—commitment, but when you think of it as an investment it becomes clear that a little time and self-reflection now will pay off big in the future.

Relationships with colleagues

OK, so you're fresh-faced, well dressed, perfectly postured and enunciating with precision. Your desk looks like the cover photo of a Feng Shui magazine. Now what? Well, now you've got to play well with others.

You have a budding relationship with your boss already, which will develop according to the natural dynamics of boss-underling relationships. But equally important are the relationships you build with other people in the company, whether it's your boss's boss, the human resource coordinator, or the receptionist. Once you've been hired the real scrutiny begins, because your new coworkers have their chance to size you up. As the newbie in the office, you will fill several functions in addition to the official duties of your new job: stranger, rookie and, sometimes, source of entertainment. Anxious yet?

Take a deep breath, wipe your palms, and repeat after us: "I have just under 10 seconds to win these people over with a stunning first impression." No problem. Those 10 seconds are critical, but you have months and even years to build relationships with these people. And while the focus of this chapter so far has been on outward appearances, a good working environment truly depends on real people bringing out the best in each other.

These tips will take you beyond the introductions and into the early months of your new job:

- **Show interest.** Be open to and interested in all the people you meet at your new job. Really listen to them, whether they're instructing you on the fine art of not jamming the copy machine or telling you about their volleyball league. Ask questions, make eye contact, try to remember specific details. People appreciate and respond to those who are sincere, engaging, and curious. Conversely, the quickest way to turn others off is to appear self-centered and aloof.

- **Be generous, but not too generous.** Give compliments, offer to buy a round of coffee, bring in treats for the staff room. But don't do any of these things too early or too much or you may come across as insincere or desperate. Acceptable for these early days: "Cool mouse pad!" "Cute kid!" "Nice spreadsheet!" Unacceptable: "You have great eyes!", "You're the best boss ever!", "Homemade cookies for everyone!"

- **Project a positive attitude.** Make sure that your net contribution to the office atmosphere is positive. Positive, energetic, professional, eager to work—all of these are traits of successful people. You might not always feel full of pep, but it's important to act like you're happy at your job and ready for business. In fact, you'll often find that acting energetic will improve your mood and actually give you the energy you need. Take stock of your small talk, too: How many of your comments and questions are "uppers" and how many are "downers"?

- **Respect your coworkers' time and expertise.** You will probably need a lot of help figuring out office procedures and protocols. Asking for guidance from coworkers is one way to get to know them. Quick requests for recommendations—the best deli, the nearest dry cleaners, a good gym—can be great conversation starters. If you need something that will take more than a few minutes of a coworker's time, however, ask if you can set up an appointment with him. That way he will know that you value his expertise and his time.

- **Accept invitations.** In these early days on the job, you want to accept as many invitations as possible. It might be tempting to do a solo lunch so you can pore over your employee manual, but the most important thing to do at this stage is to connect with the people you work with. One cautionary note, however: If the conversation during these outings with colleagues heads towards gossip, be aware of your position as the new kid on the block and maintain neutrality. The trick is to be sociable without getting sucked into a clique.

- **Connect with all players.** Everyone in the organization is important and worth knowing. Support staff (receptionists, secretaries, administrative assistants, office managers, and IT support) might have smaller paychecks than CEOs, but they are generally very powerful people in the company. Why? They have the keys (literally) to the supply closet, have access to top management, and can get you assistance when you need it fast. When you're on deadline and the copy machine goes down, you want the go-to person to be there for you. If you've cultivated a good relationship with him or her, you'll be in good shape. Also, support staff know everything about everything: They can tell you which days the boss is in a good mood and can even help you minimize a mistake if you've made one.

Winning over coworkers isn't about faking them out, but about putting your best self forward. It will help you professionally and personally if you showcase your best attributes in these early days on the job. Think about the attributes you value and admire most, then start exercising them. In other words, if you want to be poised, articulate, personable, engaged and engaging, organized, and positive, act like you already are that way. This attitude and way of being will serve you well beyond those early, first impression seconds and soon you'll see not just your impact on others, but also an impact on yourself.

Chapter 12

Understanding Your Organization

The robots of this world can judge how good a work situation is with hard, quantitative data: Add salary (X) to benefits (Y) and advancement potential (Z), then divide by commute time (C). That's it. The job is good if it pays well, offers a fancy title, and doesn't take two hours and three trains to reach. But experienced professionals, even the super computer geeks and engineers, will tell you that the feel of the organization is critical to job satisfaction. Yep, the *feel*. Or, in office speak, the organization culture.

Each organization has a unique personality, composed of its values, structures, and behaviors. When you first get to the job and begin to develop the skills and procedures that relate to your position, you'll also start to figure out your organization's culture. Most importantly, you'll begin to understand how you interact with this culture.

It's kind of like moving to a new country: Some of the traditions and expressions will seem familiar immediately, while others become clear with time and translation. Because job satisfaction directly relates to how well the organization's personality meshes with your own, you'll want to get the lay of the land early on.

Consider this chapter your guidebook to understanding your organization. We'll develop a thorough definition of organization culture, map out how you can assess your organization's personality, and offer tips on how to work with it.

Two ears, one mouth

There's an old saying that we have two ears and one mouth because we're meant to listen twice as much as we speak. Keep that saying in mind as you navigate the first weeks and months of your new job. Interviews are meant for showcasing your achievements, impressing everyone with your knowledge, and just plain selling yourself. But after the interview is over and you're the new kid on the block, it's time to show how well you adapt and work with the team, which means more watching and listening and less talking.

Here's how to start out right:

- **Watch.** Observe body language and how people in the organization interact. Where do people gather? Who are the leaders? How much space do employees give each other? Is it a heads-down environment—everyone working quietly in their cubicles or offices—or more open and collaborative? Do people take breaks? What are the work day norms—is it a 9 to 5 office that really shuts down at 5:00 p.m. or do people tend to come early, work late, and take work home?

- **Listen.** Listen to the way people communicate with each other. Do they share ideas freely? Is it an outspoken environment or more reserved? Casual or formal? How do colleagues talk about their work? How do they talk about customers, coworkers, and management?

- **Ask questions.** Learning about the organization and your new job can feel like you're drinking from a firehose, but try and absorb as much as possible without getting overwhelmed. Ask questions that will help you understand the organization better as well as your role in it. Carry a pad of paper and pencil with you so you can take good notes of everything you learn. Remember that no one expects you to know everything right off the bat so they'll see your questions as a sign of interest and a willingness to learn and adapt. It's better to ask early, too, because at some point you *will* be expected to "just know." Another way to gather valuable information is by reading— read the employee manual, organization literature, the website, and all emails that come through your inbox.

- **Implement what you learn.** Once you get the lay of the land you'll be confident you know what's expected of you. Then it's simply a matter of doing it. Look to the leaders of the organization as models of job performance. You'll find leaders—engaged, enthusiastic, and productive people—in every department and at every level, from management to support staff.

By observing the ways of others, you'll soon get a sense of how to operate successfully within the organization's environment.

Organization culture

As we mentioned in the introduction of this chapter, organization culture is a product of a combination of values, structures, and behaviors. You'll pick up on some aspects of your new workplace's culture as early as the first interview. The environment itself reveals a lot about the organization's values: From the layout of the office to the casual interactions between colleagues you'll find clues to deciphering the unwritten "codes" of culture. Here are some ideas to help guide your assessment:

- **Mission and vision.** Is there a clear, shared organization mission? Do your coworkers speak positively about the organization and its leadership? Does every employee feel invested in the future of the organization? Successful, dynamic businesses depend on a shared vision.

- **Expectations and support.** Are standards and expectations clearly defined and attainable? Do supervisors encourage and nurture employees' success on the job by giving timely and constructive feedback on their work? Are mentors available? Is there a clear evaluation/annual review system? These qualities not only foster your ongoing professional success but they also ensure that you're respected and that your contributions are valued.

- **Physical office structure.** Does the office layout say hierarchy or anarchy (or, more likely, something in-between)? An open floor plan with shared workspaces hints at a collaborative, non-hierarchical organization, while rows of cubicles surrounded by closed-door offices suggest a more stratified environment.

- **Work habits and hours.** What are the standard hours employees keep? What are the productivity expectations? Do your coworkers having working lunches and "breaks"? Are employees expected to volunteer for additional projects? Get a sense of "what everybody's doing" early on so you can adjust your pace accordingly.

- **Communication.** What are the most common modes of communication used within the office? Face to face? Email? Phone? Little sticky notes? What do you see in meetings? Does one person control the agenda or is it designed by committee? When there is tension, do the people involved treat each other respectfully? Less important are the number of disagreements around the office as the way they are resolved.

- **State of the staff room.** Is the staff room a hub for interaction or basically unused? If the lunch room is a gathering place, take advantage of the time to meet and get to know more people. Oftentimes these informal conversations are inspiring and will help you recharge. Of course, some staff rooms breed whining, or worse, gossiping. If this is the case, respectfully avoid it as much as you can.

The Importance of Participation

Some rules simply aren't outlined in the employee handbook—for instance, whether to contribute to so-and-so's baby shower gift, if you should join the softball team or not, when to go out for lunch with the group. Participate when

- The activity or event involves team building.
- Doing so will demonstrate appreciation (the holiday party, for example, takes a lot of planning and effort).
- It will allow you to sustain and establish relationships in a way you wouldn't otherwise do in the office.

- **Flexibility.** Does the organization allow or even encourage flexible work hours? Can employees job share or reduce their full time status if they want to? Remember, these options may not seem relevant to you now, but circumstances change. The more an organization recognizes that you have a life outside of work, the better.

- **Resources.** Resources might include technology, postage, food, and office supplies. How liberal is the organization with its stuff? How does one go about procuring a toner cartridge? What kind of documentation is necessary? Whatever your organization's "available resource" profile, be sensitive to norms regarding office supplies.

- **Turnover.** Do people tend to stick around or does the organization have a more fluid workforce? Of the longstanding employees, who are leaders in the organization?

A Quick Note About Alcohol...

In many organizations, the extracurriculars— holiday parties, sporting events, conferences/trade shows, BBQs and business trips, for example, involve alcohol. There are two rules here. Rule One: You should never feel obligated to drink. Rule Two: If you do drink, do so in moderation. Even if drinking is part of the organization's culture and the bosses are hosting an open-bar event, they don't really want to see employees intoxicated. And people have longer memories of drunken antics than almost any other thing a person does for the organization.

There may be other elements involved in your particular organization's personality, but these are the most common to consider as you learn to adapt to your new environment.

Email and Instant Messaging

GOOD TO KNOW

- **Tone:** Email and IM are so pervasive and easy we forget how artful some of the messages need to be. Word choice, punctuation, and capitalization (plus an emoticon or two, maybe) are the only clues your reader has to your tone. Before you write an email, think about how you can communicate this information best. Sometimes a phone call or face-to-face conversation is better. If you think an email message is the best method for the situation, do take the time to compose your messages. Also, pause before you send. And with emotional emails of any sort, pause for at least 24 hours.

- **Face-to-Face vs. Electronic Communication:** A decade ago, it would have been unheard of for next-door employees to email each other. But now it's such a creeping norm that some companies have taken the radical step of announcing no email days in order to engage employees in more face-to-face interaction. Go with the norms of your organization, but remember that in-person communication is a great way to build real relationships.

- **Privacy:** Ha. Privacy is SO early 20th century. Email only those things you'd feel comfortable posting on the staff room fridge. If your father likes to forward every off-color joke and visual that's ever circulated the Web, tell him in no uncertain terms that he needs to remove you from his contact list. Or he'll be supporting you for the rest of his life. IM is not as easy to track and monitor, but work is work, and it's best to save the personal material for home. In fact, many organizations have strict rules against using company technology for personal matters. Another thing to note: If you have a MySpace or Facebook account, be very aware that it might be viewed by someone from your workplace. Blog accordingly.

Working within your organization's culture

Your office's culture will have a profound effect on your life at work and outside of it. Expect that the organization is going to influence you at least as much as you influence it, if not more.

As with other parts of your life, some of the most important rules are the unspoken ones. Follow the ones that add to a positive environment. For example, your organization may value the holiday party, and for that reason alone, you should, too. So, if you're trying to decide whether to attend the holiday party or not, think about the impression you'll make if you do attend, or rather, the impression you'll leave behind if you don't show up. It's tough to give up a Saturday evening in December, but it's worthwhile and will likely mean a lot to those you work with.

Some norms, of course, are better broken or ignored. Even the most positive workplaces might contain a group that thrives on gossip, undermining, or other detrimental behaviors. Of course you'll want to avoid spreading gossip or getting too close with anyone known for spreading gossip. If you detect a clique, be friendly with the members in a way that is respectful but keeps you a safe distance from becoming part of the group. That way you won't end up inadvertently alienating yourself from colleagues outside the clique. Other bad habits to avoid include complaining, bad-mouthing, and lax expense accounting. If the norms at your organization are too far afield of your best judgment, you might want to consider a job switch.

While there are guidelines and tools to help you assess your organization's personality, there's no simple, objective formula to predict how soon you'll feel like "one of the natives." If you're lucky, you've landed in an organization that feels like a good match, a place where you can learn and grow comfortably. However, even an imperfect match can be instructive. When you learn to work well within a challenging culture, you hone skills that are incredibly helpful in the long run. Keep your overall personal and professional goals in mind. You'll be able to learn from all experiences, and apply the knowledge you've gained to a long and rewarding career.

Chapter 13

Realistic Expectations

You've heard of sticker shock and culture shock, but here's a new condition you should know about: Reality shock. Reality shock is the state many recent graduates find themselves in a week or so into their first job, when their expectations for the job collide head-on with the reality of the organization's expectations of them. So if your eyes ache from the flash of the copier machine and the blur of entering data, know this: Everyone starts somewhere.

Open up a copy of *Forbes* or *Fortune* and scan the pages. All those high-powered executives? You can bet that almost every one of them put in their time filing, copying, faxing, and doing all the tasks considered, well, boring. The vast majority of professionals paid their dues in the early years of their career. However, articles and stories that celebrate successful people often gloss over the boring stuff and head straight for the critical plays, breakthroughs, and stellar accomplishments. We want to hear about someone collating and three-hole punching about as much as we want to hear Uncle Dave's "when I was a kid I walked three miles each way to school" stories. And when most of what we know about the working world is based on television, magazine profiles, or even textbooks, it's not surprising that most of us suffer from at least a little reality shock.

We hope this chapter will help you set realistic expectations for yourself, understand the most common causes of reality shock, and see what you're doing now as one step in a successful career.

The importance of having realistic expectations

Did you ever get so excited for a gathering or a big trip that when the actual event came it was anticlimactic? Not that it was bad, but it just wasn't what you imagined somehow. That gap between anticipated excitement and reality can be a bummer. And even if you are generally an optimistic and motivated person, it's not uncommon to get so excited by the job search and hiring process that when you start the daily work it seems, well, just like work. Contributing to this feeling is the great sense of accomplishment you get when you graduate: Here I am world! Qualified! Degreed! Skilled! Energetic! Master of my field! And then someone asks you to change the toner.

If you feel this reality shock you are by no means alone. In fact, the most common complaint of new hires after two weeks on the job is that it isn't what they expected. The good news is it's no longer a complaint after two months on the job. The message here is clear: Give it time. In the meantime, learn about the most frequent causes of new job dissatisfaction.

Employer needs/new employee needs

It's natural to come out of school ready to "hit the ground running" and prove yourself. You are smart and motivated and eager to become an integral part of the team. Your employer probably hired you for all of these reasons and will ultimately be happy to let you work to your fullest potential. However, it's possible that your needs and your employer's needs in these early days are not the same. It's not necessarily that they are at odds with each other, but more that they're operating at different speeds. You want to run with your talents and take an active role in the organization; your supervisor needs to train you and evaluate your skills and level of commitment. The organization is investing time, energy, and money in you and needs to see evidence that you're invested, too.

You can expect, then, that the early days will involve training and sometimes repetitive tasks. Employers generally like to ease new employees into the scene and provide them with background information as well as a chance to get used to the office norms. Some organizations' training programs are very comprehensive, designed to teach every aspect of the organization to every employee. (A restaurant analogy is helpful here: The chef should know how to wash dishes even if her job description focuses on food preparation.)

Whatever the reason for your new-hire job duties, remember they hired you because they're really busy and need help. Right now you might be stapling and changing the occasional ink cartridge, but once they see you care about the job you'll be on your way to doing other things that are more in line with your goals. Here are some things to keep in mind on these early days on the job:

- **Everyone starts somewhere.** Even the CEO has spent time copying, collating, and entering data.

- **Demonstrate initiative.** Volunteer for projects and tasks. Your main goal at this point, after all, is to get to know the ins and outs of your new organization.

- **Be positive.** Your positive outlook and willingness to contribute *will* be noticed.

- **Do a good job.** This one might be intuitive, but it bears repeating. Whatever your assigned task, do it carefully and do it well. Every action should convey your attention to details and ability to produce quality work.

- **Be patient with yourself.** It can be frustrating to learn the ropes at a new job. It's typical to make mistakes in these early days. On top of that, you may feel slow and inefficient. Don't worry. You will get the hang of it. Focus on one task at a time.

New Employee Needs	Organization Needs (supervisor and coworkers)
Challenging Tasks	To know that the new employee is competent
Autonomy	Evidence that new employee is trustworthy and understands his/her function in the organization
To feel he/she belongs and is liked	Evidence new employee is making an effort to fit in and respects others' time and space

If you need to ask about the tasks you've been assigned, try to begin the question with an "I understand" statement. For example, say, "I understand the value of this training process, but I'm curious about when I can expect to transition to other tasks." This will show your supervisor that you're ready to move on without making it seem like you're resistant to instruction.

So far we've assumed you might be dealing with the reality shock that comes from not being given what you think is meaningful, challenging work. There are other types of shock, though. Sometimes you'll land in an organization that is so slammed with work that you get all sorts of interesting, high-stakes projects—and no training. A situation like this can make even the most competent person feel completely overwhelmed.

You want cream and sugar with that?

Collin S., now a journalist for a national publication, was shocked when his supervisor asked him to go on a coffee run on his second day on the job. "Here I was, fresh out of college, having won all these awards and accolades in school and my boss wanted me to be the coffee boy! I was furious. Also kind of embarrassed because the errand was like a red flag: 'New guy. Low man on campus.' But I did it anyway, of course. What I realized after working there for a few weeks was that everyone took turns getting coffee or running out for sandwiches. Sure, they asked me that day because I was the new guy, but it didn't have nearly the significance I thought it did."

To make the most of it, ask questions of available coworkers, and try to learn by example. It's a challenge to face such a steep learning curve, but it can be incredibly rewarding in the end. In this case, your employer's need—to get someone who will learn and produce fast—might be a great jump start to your career with the organization. And chances are, you'll end up feeling like an integral player in the organization's success.

Other common causes of reality shock

In addition to the gap between the employer's needs and your own, there may be some other unexpected realities of work. Following are some of the most common surprises:

- **Bosses.** Bosses are more demanding than college professors, and in the workplace success is often judged simply on results. This is in contrast to college, where success is often evaluated according to product and process. In other words, a professor might care if you've invested a lot of time and energy into a paper or project, but a boss is just going to look at the final product.

- **Salary.** Many graduates overestimate their initial salary potential as well as the frequency and rate of promotions. Raises, too, are on average much lower than television or corporate lore would have us believe. Your workplace's human resources department is a good place to start asking what standard promotion and salary practices are for that organization. You can also look online for regional norms if you want to get an outside perspective.

- **Workspace.** Another sometimes jarring reality is the workspace you'll have when you first start. A cubicle, a corner of the staff room, a shared table. If you're disappointed with your placement, just keep in mind that your status is a function of how you see yourself, not where you sit or what computer you've been assigned.

- **Work hours.** Other common surprises include time demands. You might be hired for what seems like a forty-hour a week job, but end up putting in many more hours learning the ropes and doing what it takes to complete the tasks you've been given. You will get more efficient as time goes on, but it's also possible that the organization survives on lots of people working lots of hours. Or even just a few people working lots and lots of hours. If that's the case, you'll either get acclimated to the time spent on the job or decide to shift gears.

- **Fitting in.** If one of the other feelings you experience is a lack of a sense of belonging, rest assured that this is typical at first. Your new coworkers are busy and won't necessarily go out of their way to meet the new person. But take heart. With time you'll get to know each other and the relationships will develop naturally. Do what you can to connect with them: Ask them questions about their interests, invite them to join you for lunch, and accept invitations they extend to you.

Whatever your experiences in the first weeks and months of your new job, try to keep your ultimate goals in mind. At some point in the not-so-distant future, you'll be doing the work you want to be doing.

Chapter 14

Go Beyond Average

Average. Even the word is boring. Kind of nasally and slow, like a whine. It's no surprise, then, that no one wants to be average. We want below average cholesterol and above average intelligence, but even that seems a little dull. Who wants to go to a restaurant or a doctor with just an "above average" reputation? Who wants to be labeled "above average"? Bleh. It's as good as saying "not excellent."

So let's get rid of that word right here. In your work life you want to be way beyond average. Not even in the same realm. Instead, you'll be excellent. Superior. Remarkable. Now, in school a person needs simply to meet the standard in order to pass the class. But in work if you just meet the standard you could end up with job paralysis. Instead, you want to advance your knowledge and experience (and, yes, your salary) so you need to go beyond the basic job description on a regular basis. A dynamic, fulfilling career is composed of many daily decisions to exceed expectations.

The cool thing is that starting your job with the mission of proving to both your supervisors and yourself that you've got the right stuff will instill a habit of excellence. You'll become so accustomed to welcoming challenges and doing your best that remarkable job performance will be your norm. And you'll find that the energy you give will come back to you.

Now, the advice in this chapter is common sense, the stuff of Abe Lincoln stories and more than one commencement address. But there's a reason these tips are repeated in various forms by successful people: Going beyond expectations is what separates the "average" and "above average" professional from the "very successful" one.

Work a full day

We know, we know. This one seems painfully obvious. However, even though conventional wisdom says to work a full day at your job if you want to excel, managers still report that many employees arrive a little late and leave a little early. And take a lot of breaks. Now, circadian rhythm and psychological studies may show that flexible hours plus a nap in the middle of the day boosts productivity and efficiency, but let's just say that most of the working world hasn't caught up to this way of thinking.

People notice if you arrive late and leave early, and they really, really notice if you show up for a meeting with sleep creases on your face. No matter how much you're actually getting done, timeliness can't be underestimated. If you get to the office early and leave a little late, you'll establish yourself as someone who is committed and hardworking. And that's the kind of getting noticed you want.

Do your job well

Whatever you're doing, take pride in your work. Two sayings come to mind here: "All work is meaningful" and "Way leads onto way." And while such words might sound pat when you're doing double data entry and extreme filing, they're true. We all start somewhere, and if it's in document shredding, well, be a fast, thorough (and ethical!) shredder. Write a book about it—*Zen and the Art of Document Shredding*—or a comedy routine. Or come up with a better method of shredding and patent it. Or simply finish the shredding early and volunteer to take on a task that will really challenge you and showcase your talents.

Way Leads Onto Way

We've all seen the movies of ascent in the corporate world. Young man starts off sorting letters in the mail room, and with a little ingenuity, maneuvering, and help from a kindly administrative assistant, he becomes CEO within a few years. It's fiction of course, and sexist, but it reveals the basic formula for obtaining the job you want: **Ideas plus initiative plus help from the right people = success.**

Take the initiative

One great way to demonstrate your willingness to work hard as well as your yet-to-be-fully-revealed capabilities is to take the initiative and volunteer for projects, committees, and additional training. These volunteer efforts could mean taking on gigantic projects—rewriting a computer program, for instance, or creating a style manual—or even offering assistance with the little tasks that aren't glamorous but simply need to get done, like binding a report or running copies.

Taking on tasks outside your job requirements, whether those tasks are challenging or remedial, will help you learn more about the organization, develop your skills, and establish strong relationships with your supervisors and colleagues.

Make the most of your mistakes

Superior job performance includes dealing with

Treat Every Project Like a Raise Depends on It

Every day, and with every task, ask yourself if you're working to your full potential. Sure, you're **To Do!** past tryouts (the interviews and probationary period) and have made the team, but you still need to prove your worth to the organization on a daily basis. This will benefit you and the organization you work for. People who treat every task and project like a raise depends on it tend to have a higher rate of job satisfaction and fulfillment. And, on top of it all, they are more likely to earn rewards like . . . promotions and raises.

mistakes in a constructive way. The below average employee covers up or blows off mistakes; the average employee minimizes his or her mistakes by passing or maybe "sharing" the buck; the not-even-in-the-realm-of-average, excellent employee takes responsibility for his or her mistakes, learns from them, and moves on. It's not a question *if* you'll make mistakes but how you'll deal with them when you do. If you're up front about your role in an error, reflect on it, and self-correct, the mistake itself won't be nearly as memorable as the lasting impression of your integrity and dedication to doing your job right.

Contribute positively to the organization

All employees contribute to the company, but not all add to it. Compelling paradox, but what does it mean? Good question and, like all good questions, the answer lies within. Get in the habit of asking yourself if you are adding positively to the environment. Before making a statement or asking a question in a meeting, for instance, ask yourself, "Is this going to add and help or will it distract from the purpose? Am I offering solutions or problems?" When talking with others in the staff room, ask yourself, "Am I adding something positive here?"

Whatever the phrasing of your self-reflections, the root questions are *What are my intentions?* and *What are the possible implications of this statement/action?* Checking in with yourself on a regular basis will help you maintain a consistently positive role in your company. We're not saying, however, that you need to be a yes man, or woman. On the contrary, successful people often need to question the status quo or their colleagues' and supervisor's ideas. But if your intentions and methods are good, you'll know how to add in a productive, meaningful way.

Take care of yourself...

...or you're no help to anyone else. Being excellent all the time takes a lot of energy. In order to do your work well you need to take care of yourself, too. So while we recommend volunteering for projects and committees, and certainly advise you to expect to dedicate many hours on and off the job working, it's also very important to take care of your personal needs. Sleep, for example, is not an optional activity. Being your best at work means being your best, period. Alert. Focused. Personable. Even fun. So if you do choose to sign up for an additional project, do it well. Don't overextend yourself—you want to come across as professional, competent, and motivated rather than frazzled.

If you're lucky you're surrounded by supervisors and colleagues who share a desire to be way beyond average. In your company, the norm might be excellence and so "meeting the standard" means working at a very high level all the time. Such work environments can be incredibly supportive of both the individual's and the company's needs, inspiring every employee to work beyond his or her potential. Whatever your actual job circumstances, set high expectations for your own performance and you'll always be better off for having done so.

Chapter 15

What Your College Has to Offer You Now

Remember those long nights of studying and the way your eyes glazed over the pages of a text book at 2:00 a.m.? Remember how your hands cramped as you scribbled and scrawled over every possible surface of the test booklet during an exam? Well, for most graduates, those trials are over.

The tests and papers are filed away and you have one simple task remaining: Right click, add bookmark. No aches and pains. Just a simple keystroke or two and you enter into a world of opportunity, a world where experts offer you free or next-to-free financial advice, a world where everyone wants to help you find the job of your dreams and can actually help make that happen, a world of drastic discounts on auto insurance and even pizza. That's right...you have just bookmarked your alumni association's webpage.

Many people don't realize or take advantage of one of college's most important resources: its deep pool of graduates. If you're not connecting with them yet you're in for a very pleasant surprise when you find out how much you actually got for all the work you did in college. First a degree and now access to all sorts of cool services as well as a dynamic network of alumni.

If the classroom represents *What* you know, your alumni association represents *Who* you know. Any successful person will tell you that an education can open a lot of doors for you, but connections can open even more. One of the primary functions of the alumni association, after all, is to create and support a social and professional community based on a common background. It's difficult to overstate the benefits of taking part in such a community. In this chapter we'll tell you about the networking opportunities and other services alumni organizations provide and how you can tap into them.

Networking

The primary purpose of alumni groups is to nurture graduates' ties to their alma mater. And while the buildings, quads, and fountains of the college campus continue to inspire a sense of belonging in the graduate, it's the people who make a school's environment truly rich and lasting. Alumni organizations extend the experience by offering graduates frequent and varied opportunities to connect with other alumni. Some people are motivated by the social aspects of such a group, others motivated by the career-boosting advantages. Most seek a combination of both. Here are some of the networking possibilities available:

- **Alumni clubs/chapters.** Alumni associations usually have smaller regional clubs/chapters so graduates can get to know other alumni who live nearby. The only prerequisites for belonging, besides being an alum, are signing up and, in some cases, paying dues. The more active of these groups might organize charity events, college recruitment efforts, lectures and seminars, book groups, opera outings, holiday parties, tailgate parties, and other sports-centered events. Some of the less active clubs might be content to host an occasional alumni happy hour at the local restaurant. It's a good idea to check out at least a few of the events—you might see some old friends from school and you could end up meeting some new ones. Also, these casual get togethers are a great way to network on a regular basis.

Benefits of Networking

What, exactly, are the benefits of networking? Why go to a meet-and-greet when you could be hanging out at home watching your favorite TV show? If you tap into an effective and supportive network, you'll...

- **Discover valuable resources, new methods and practice in your field, and unique approaches to problems.**
- **Exchange ideas with people in and outside of your practice in order to enlarge your understanding.**
- **Get advice from experienced professionals.**
- **Get inspired by meeting energetic, creative people (after all, none of you is staying home watching TV).**
- **Increase your visibility if you're building up a business or clientele.**
- **Get leads on new clients, job opportunities, employees, etc.**

- **Shared interest groups.** Do you want to work for a service organization in a developing country? Are you starting a technology business? Do you ski? Your alumni website can point you to all sorts of ways you can connect with like-minded people. You might find an online discussion group centered on your area of study or, in some cases, an alumni chapter in your town that's made up of people who majored in the same field. These groups can provide valuable support as you take on new challenges. They can also, of course, introduce you to others who might know someone who knows someone who's looking to invest in a promising new company. Or someone who knows of a perfect job opportunity for you. Or—even better—someone who knows how you can score tickets to a sold-out show.

- **Mentor programs.**

Networking Etiquette

Here are some rules for networking with class:

- **Remember: Person First.** Approach people as interesting individuals, not job titles. The person you introduce yourself to at the meet-and-greet might end up being a great client, but only if they feel respected and liked.

- **Conversation Sells More Than Selling.** In other words, engage with people authentically and know when to talk shop and when to talk about other things.

- **Respect Others' Time.** Everyone is busy. Be graciously aware of the other person's time constraints. Also, send a thank you card when someone does you the favor of giving up their time to help you.

Some associations match experienced and novice professionals. The volunteer mentor gets the satisfaction of helping an up-and-coming young person establish him or herself. The up-and-coming young person (that's you) gets the benefit of years of wisdom and experience at the beginning of his or her career. (Also, said newly graduated professional might meet a mentor who's looking for a bright, capable hire—at double the mentee's current salary).

- **Singles groups.** Another important aspect of life after graduation for many people is meeting interesting singles. Some associations now offer singles activities—whitewater rafting, anyone?—as well as password-protected message boards and similar sites.

Whatever your field of interest or motivation for getting involved with your association, networking invariably broadens one's horizons and prospects. Another way to tap into the your alumni association is through the services it offers.

Services

Many of the services available serve the dual purpose of networking, but we include them separately because networking is not their primary function. The following is a list of services your alumni organization might offer:

- **Career planning services.** From password-protected job boards to access to informational interviews with alumni, the career planning services available through some schools' associations are phenomenal. There are workshops, individual career counseling, and even resume tutorials and critiques. Some colleges charge for these services, but the fees are minimal and a great investment for the cost.

- **Relocation support.** If you're relocating it's a good idea to check with the alumni chapter in your new region. You might find people eager to guide you through the ins and outs of your new location, whether that means introducing you to a great real estate agent or giving you tips on the local scene. Some national alumni associations even have programs to assist spouses and children with their relocation issues.

- **Business development.** You can post information about your business, recruit employees, and even get a grant or loan, depending on your alumni association. People starting new companies, by the way, can get a lot of free advice and press by simply contacting other alumni.

- **Travel.** Want to attend a Civil War lecture at the site of a significant battle? Feel like going to Italy for a few weeks this spring? Again, you might be surprised at how many cool travel opportunities your association offers. As a large organization, it has the clout to recruit expert guides and lecturers as well as the buying power to qualify for discounted travel expenses. (That doesn't mean that all alumni travel is en masse.) And if for some reason your college doesn't offer the cool seminars and group tours, your membership in the local chapter can probably garner you a personal discount on airfare or travel-related expenses.

- **Continuing education.** For those of you who never wanted to leave college, take heart! You can keep learning and this time you don't need to suffer the writer's block and hand cramps of the finals weeks of old. If you live close to campus you may be eligible to audit classes. Or you might find that your local chapter recruits great lecturers for their meetings. Some schools post free online lectures for alumni. Others host research databases. There are countless ways you can continue your education and the first place to look for opportunities is the association webpage

- **Discounts.** Oh, yes. This alone is worth those tuition checks. Here's a noncomprehensive overview of discounts we found while perusing a variety of alumni associations: pizza, luxury cars, life insurance, eye exams, carpet cleaning, airfare, credit card interest rates, auto insurance, pet food, college credits. Basically, if it's something you pay for you might find you can pay less for it by flashing your alum ID card.

Whew. That's a lot of goods for a simple action. Right click, bookmark, and all of a sudden you're basking in the sun in the mountains of Italy, networking by email with a big time venture capitalist, discussing everything from investments to the current basketball season. OK, so maybe we overstate the benefits of this resource, the alumni association. On the other hand, where else will you find an organization that offers access to prime career development services as well as frequent networking opportunites (and, of course, great tailgate parties).

Chapter 16

What You Have to Offer Your College

One of the great pleasures in life is watching the new wing on the student union building take shape with your name etched in the stone cornice above the entryway. You know that generations of students will benefit from your generosity. Other satisfying ways to contribute to your alma mater are establishing a professorship or donating an electron microscope.

That time will come. For the present, you're probably more concerned with monthly expenses than architectural drawings of your legacy. However, every philanthropist starts somewhere; what matters is not the size of the contribution or the form it takes, but the very act of contributing.

Recent graduates may be shocked by how soon solicitations show up from their college alumni association. The cap and gown are barely put away when the first brochure appears in the mailbox. Or the friendly voice sounds on the telephone: "Hello, Ms. So-and-so? This is Karly from Your University." After you realize the student representative is really calling for you and not your mother, the shock kicks in: This is my new world. Adult. Alum. Pledge drives.

But then you realize it's not about giving in to or dodging from work-study students. It's about staying connected with your college and shaping its future. You know how you benefit from maintaining contact (see Chapter 15); here are some ways you can give back to the college community, and only a couple of them relate to money.

Maintaining contact

We outlined some of the perks of staying in touch with your college and alumni association in the previous chapter. Your college benefits from this continued relationship, too. First, even your basic personal information and updates can add to the larger statistical picture that informs program direction and funding: Who graduates from which department, what they do post-graduation, how they apply their degree to their lives outside of school, etc. Also, and more importantly, your continued involvement builds on the network that supports current and former students as well as school departments and programs. You rely on the network and the network relies on you.

What's the best way to stay in contact? Well, the simplest way is by filling out and sending back the occasional forms that ask for your most recent information. Another easy way is to join the local alumni club/chapter and commit to attending a few events a year. If you want to be more involved, consider volunteering for your college or alumni association.

Mentoring

Mentoring is a powerful way to stay connected to your college: You get the pleasure of sharing your skills and expertise, and the beneficiaries of your efforts get the assistance they need and will someday pass it on to others. Mentor programs vary in structure and size from college to college, but they all focus on connecting experienced professionals with up-and-coming professionals. Once you feel established in your career, think about the guidance you had (or would like to have had) as a student. Then, volunteer in a capacity that fits your knowledge and, of course, schedule. You might meet one-on-one with a student to discuss new research and opportunities in your shared field of study or you could assist students by providing informational interviews. Another helpful service you might offer is critiquing resumes and cover letters. If you're interested in career coaching, some alumni associations offer mentors training in how to help guide students in that area.

Alumni Mentors...

GOOD TO KNOW

- Share their knowledge and expertise
- Offer guidance with internship opportunities and job searches
- Provide informational interviews
- Help connect students with professional organizations
- Give students on-the-job experience
- Coach students on interview and presentation skills
- Speak to large or small groups at high schools or other organizations about the college

Mentoring is a rewarding and flexible method of contributing to your college community. If you have an hour a week you can take part in an online Q and A or offer advice on a career search message board. If you have more time you can take on a larger role in the alumni network. The results of your energies won't be written in stone on the new student union building, but they will be just as long-lasting.

Volunteer work

Are you itching to do something meaningful outside of your job? There comes a point in most people's careers when they're satisfied with the work they're doing but just need to add a little more to the greater community. If you fit this profile, consider contributing time to your college. As with mentoring, the extent of your involvement is up to you: Have an afternoon? Help out with the annual fund drive. Have a day? Help out at the new student orientation. Have grant-writing experience? Well, there's no end to the ways your school could put that to work.

Geography is not an issue, either. Even if you live far from your alma mater you can help out with recruitment or other efforts not tied to campus. Consider serving on the alumni association board of directors, for instance, or serving in a leadership position for your regional council/chapter.

Financial support

So far we've gone over some of the ways you can support your college family without touching—much less breaking—the bank. Now let's talk about how you can give financial support even as you're starting your career. We'll call it "philanthropy on a budget."

First, look to the easy ways to make frequent, smaller gifts to your alma mater. Some schools are affiliated with phone plans and credit cards that give a percentage of each expense to the institution. These plans might work for you, though it's important to do the math and see if you could save more by using another credit card but maybe put part of those saved dollars toward an annual gift to your alumni association. Other minor expenses include things like paying dues to your annual alumni dues (not all schools have dues) and purchasing school-related license plates.

If you have more to give, whether it's $10 or $100 or $1,000 or more, you have a few options for *how* to give.

Why contribute? *Consider This ...*

- You want up-and-coming students to have the same opportunities you had.

- Your gift has exponential potential. A strong base support builds on itself—colleges that can demonstrate they are already well-supported are more likely to secure even bigger contributions and grants.

- As your college and its reputation grows, so does the value of your degree.

Where does the money go? *Good To Know*

- Teaching and learning programs
- Student research support
- Scholarships and grants
- Recruitment efforts
- Orientation programs
- Chairs and professorships
- Facility and technology upgrades

These include:

- **Designated gifts:** You direct your gift to the department or program of your choosing.

- **Unrestricted gifts:** You let the school—administration, department heads, or alumni association—decide the best use of your gift.

- **Matching gifts:** Before you contribute, ask your human resources department if your company matches gifts. This is a great way to leverage your contributions.

Whatever you do, remember to keep your receipts so you can take advantage of all eligible tax deductions.

You'll find that there are many perks associated with giving back to your college family. From free sporting event tickets to access to college-owned housing around the world, your alumni association has come up with clever ways to keep you engaged and involved with your alma mater. And, you may even get tax deductions or more visibility, which can be very helpful if, say, you're an independent agent. When you stay connected you win and the college community—present and future—wins.